BRIT   S

L

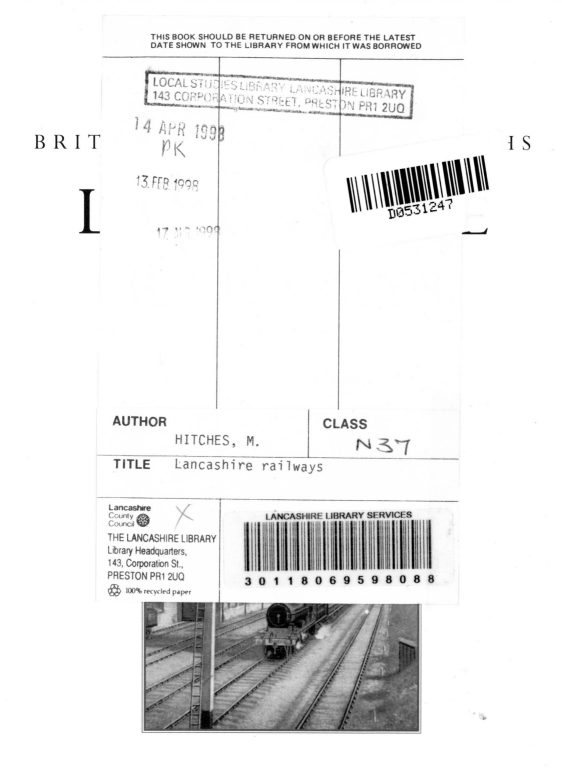

SUTTON PUBLISHING LIMITED

06959808

Sutton Publishing Limited
Phoenix Mill · Thrupp · Stroud
Gloucestershire · GL5 2BU

First published 1996

Copyright © Mike Hitches & Jim Roberts 1996

British Library Cataloguing in Publication Data
A catalogue record for this book is available from the British Library.

ISBN 0-7509-0979-X

Typeset in 10/12 Perpetua.
Typesetting and origination by
Sutton Publishing Limited.
Printed in Great Britain by
Ebenezer Baylis, Worcester.

To Sheila, Peter, John and Kay

CONTENTS

INTRODUCTION

Lancashire has long been the centre of the cotton industry – indeed, it was said that the county's cotton mills clothed the Empire. Raw cotton was imported first from India and later from the southern USA, all arriving at Liverpool for onward transit to the cotton mills of Manchester and other Lancashire towns. Finished cotton goods were then sent back to Liverpool for export all over the world. Thus, transport was essential within the county.

Until the middle of the eighteenth century raw materials and finished goods were transported by packhorses, which were slow and expensive, until replaced by canals which could carry bulk loads at much lower rates. It is not surprising, therefore, that having proved viable in the north-east of England, embryo railway companies looked to Lancashire for development where, if successful, the pickings would be rich indeed. The county was at the forefront of railway development from the very earliest days, and Liverpool business financed railway construction outside Lancashire, being involved principally in the Grand Junction Railway which linked the county with the industrial West Midlands town of Birmingham and, via the London and Birmingham Railway, the capital. It could be argued that it was Lancashire which gave railways, as we know them, to the world.

The Lancashire railway system also benefited in other ways. Rich deposits of coal in areas like Wigan brought additional railway business. The docks of Liverpool produced rail traffic for import and export of goods across Britain, as well as passenger business in connection with ocean liners, most of which used the port. Local traffic was also generated as sailors and dock workers used the railways to reach the numerous quays. As the railway network spread, seaside resorts sprang up on the Lancashire coast at places like Blackpool, Southport and Morecambe. Many thousands of Lancastrians flocked here, mostly by rail, during the summer 'Wakes Weeks', the annual holiday from the cotton mills. Morecambe, and later nearby Heysham, was also a port for packet boats to the Isle of Man and Belfast, which generated even more railway passenger traffic. Manchester was also an important centre with, like Liverpool, direct passenger links with London and Birmingham, along with numerous local services to its suburbs and other Lancashire towns.

Many of the Lancashire towns served by the railways became famous the world over not just for cotton but because of the professional football teams based there. Some of them are still renowned like Liverpool (and Everton), Manchester (United and City), and Blackburn (Rovers). Others, whose star status has waned, include Burnley, Oldham (Athletic), Preston (North End), Bolton (Wanderers), Accrington (Stanley) and Stanley Matthews' Blackpool. In the golden days of these latter clubs, the teams would have travelled by train to away fixtures and visiting teams would have arrived by rail.

Several small companies developed the Lancashire railway network, all of which amalgamated to form larger organizations. The L&M and GJR, along with others, were formed into the mighty London & North Western Railway, while the Manchester & Leeds and East Lancashire Railway became the Lancashire & Yorkshire Railway. The Midland Railway also had a route through the county, to Morecambe. At the 1923 'Grouping', these companies became constituents of the London, Midland & Scottish Railway, the LMS having control of most of the county. The LNER was also present, through the Great Central Railway's line from Marylebone to Manchester, and lines into Oldham. Other companies in Lancashire included the Cheshire Lines Committee, whose main line from Chester (Northgate) terminated at Manchester (Central), and the North Staffordshire Railway.

Lancashire was at the forefront in development of new forms of traction, away from steam. The Lancashire & Yorkshire Railway proposed electric traction on its line between Liverpool and Southport in 1902. A service began in 1904 following its successful application on the Mersey Railway which linked Birkenhead, on the Wirral, with Liverpool, passing under the River Mersey. Between 1905 and 1913, electrification was extended to Bury and Ormskirk. All of these lines used a 630 volt DC third-rail system. The Midland Railway line between Lancaster, Morecambe and Heysham was electrified, opening in April 1908, using the 6,600 volt AC system with collection from overhead wires. This line was to become the 'test-bed' for British Railways' high voltage 25 kv main line electrification scheme from 1956. Electrification of the London–Midland Region's BR main line between Manchester and Crewe, using the 25 kv overhead system after successful trials on the Morecambe line, was completed in September 1960 – another 'first' for Lancashire.

After the First World War, Lancashire's cotton industry went into decline as traditional export markets disappeared, having been forced to produce their own textiles while Lancashire's mills went into war time munitions production. Matters were made even more difficult when these same countries sent cheap cotton goods for import into the UK, which led to mass unemployment in the county. The 1920s and '30s brought misery to mill workers' families living on the 'dole', leading to severe loss of freight and passenger revenue for the railways. Worse was to follow, with the closure of Lancashire coal mines and the decline in the importance of the Port of Liverpool as major liner companies transferred their ships to Southampton. The Second World War improved the situation as Lancashire once again geared up to war production, but this only masked real economic problems in the county. The post-war years saw the final demise of the cotton industry, coal mining and ocean liner traffic. In time these old industries were replaced by new ones, but they looked to road haulage rather than the railways. Passenger traffic also went into decline thanks to bus and coach competition. Rapid expansion of private car ownership from the 1960s also had a devastating effect on passenger revenues. The railways, under state ownership since 1948, responded by introducing new diesel and electric trains and met with some success in attracting back passengers. Despite these moderate successes, stations and lines were closed within Lancashire, most as a result of Dr Beeching's infamous 1963 'Reshaping Report'. Today, the main trunk routes between Liverpool, Manchester, Birmingham (New Street) and London (Euston) remain open, and have been fully electrified since the mid-1960s, but many branches have gone, never to return. However, development of tramways in Manchester suggests that railways will still play an important part in the future of Lancashire.

In this book we hope that we have captured the great days of the railways in Lancashire when busy cotton mills, whose chimneys dominated the skyline of many towns, sent products from the county by rail and when trains were the premier way to travel. Above all, we hope that our efforts bring much enjoyment.

THE LIVERPOOL &
MANCHESTER RAILWAY

Uniting the important seaport of Liverpool with the cotton capital, Manchester, the 30 mile long Liverpool &
Manchester Railway was the first true 'Inter-City' line to be built. It was also the first railway to use steam traction
throughout. Inspiration for constructing a railway between the two major cities was the need to transport raw cotton
from Liverpool docks to the spinning and weaving mills in the Manchester area, and to take finished textiles back to
Liverpool for export. Bulk transport of cotton had been provided by a canal system that had existed since the mid-
eighteenth century, but with the system fully utilized there was little incentive to improve on slow delivery times.
Indeed, raw cotton from the southern USA could spend longer on dockside wharves after import than it took sailing
ships to cross the Atlantic.

The Stockton & Darlington Railway, opened in 1825, had proved the value of a railway for bulk shipment of
freight (in their case it was coal), and directors of the embryo L&M approached the north-eastern company about
engineering a line of their own. They were told to make their own arrangements with George Stephenson, who had
engineered the S&D. Stephenson surveyed a route in 1824, but resistance from canal owners led to the Bill for the line
being thrown out by parliament. In 1825 a new survey was carried out and canal owners bought off, and the railway
company obtained its Act.

The line was built as a double-track railway from the outset on a gauge of 4 ft 8½ in (destined to become the
standard for all of the British network), with the same distance provided between the inner running rails so that
unusually wide loads could be carried over the inner rails. This was to prove too narrow a gap with fatal consequences.
On opening day, 15 September 1830, the guest of honour was the Prime Minister, the famous Duke of Wellington.
Liverpool MP, William Huskisson, who had not seen eye-to-eye with the Duke, went over to patch up differences with
him while the train was taking water at Parkside. As they were talking, Mr Huskisson was caught between the Prime
Minister's carriage and the Rocket loco which was hauling a train on the other track. He suffered crush injuries and
died at Eccles that night, the first railway casualty.

The L & M, with termini at Crown Street, Liverpool, and Liverpool Road, Manchester, rapidly became a
commercial success with both freight and passengers being quickly attracted to the line, to the detriment of other forms
of transport. Within three months of opening over half of the stagecoaches which had plied between the two cities had
disappeared from the roads, and by the end of 1830, after only 3½ months in operation, the company reported profits
of £14,432.

The L & M directors were content to concentrate on the main line only, but other companies made railway
connections to it. For example, the Bolton & Leigh Railway opened a line from the L & M to Bolton (Great Moor
Street) and the canal at Leigh in 1831. The most important line to connect with the L & M, however, was the Grand
Junction Railway which opened in 1837. It gave a railway link between Liverpool, Manchester and the fast growing
West Midlands industrial town of Birmingham. Only a year later the two north-west cities had a direct connection
with the capital when the London & Birmingham Railway was opened.

Crown Street station, Liverpool, proved inadequate for demand and the L & M was authorized to build a tunnel
from Edge Hill to Lime Street, a new station opening at Lime Street on 15 August 1836, in time for use by the GJR.
The GJR had its own loco works at Edge Hill, on the L & M, until moving to Crewe in 1843.

The L & M, GJR and L & B became part of the London & North Western Railway in 1846, and the first 'Inter-
City' line is still part of the British railway network, handling fast electric trains. It remains as a tribute to those far-
thinking men of pre-Victorian England.

George Stephenson's famous 0–2–2 locomotive *Rocket*, winner of the L & M Rainhill Trials which commenced on 6 October 1829. As the L & M neared completion in 1828, the directors were still undecided about what sort of power should be used to run trains over the line. They were not totally convinced that steam locomotives were ideal for the railway, many still favouring the use of stationary engines placed at intervals along the line, with trains being hauled by cables. Unfortunately, some fifty-four of these stationary engines would be required to haul trains and one single breakdown could paralyse the whole route. Purchasing and installing these engines would also cost a huge amount of money, an important consideration at this time. George Stephenson advocated the use of steam locos, not surprising as he was very much involved in their construction. The directors were not really convinced, but still sent deputations to look at steam engines working on railways that then existed in the north-east of England. Eventually, it was decided that series of loco trials over 2½ miles of level track at Rainhill should be run; the winner would receive a prize of £500 and the engine would be purchased by the L & M. The trials ran for a week, in front of an average of 15,000 spectators, with five entrants vying for the prize. The ultimate winner, *Rocket*, was joined by Timothy Hackworth's *Sans Pareil*, *Novelty* entered by John Braithwaite and John Ericcson (which had been produced in seven weeks and looked like a tea urn on wheels), Timothy Burstall's *Perseverance* (which fell off a road vehicle as it was transported to Rainhill) and *Cyclopede* (a light cart which contained a treadmill worked by two horses) entered by T. Brandreth. The latter two locos were no more than 'also rans', while *Novelty* had no staying power despite running at speeds of up to 28 m.p.h. and *Sans Pareil* leaked. *Rocket* hauled 12½ tons at a steady 12 m.p.h. over all its ten runs without difficulty and ran light at up to 29 m.p.h. Thus, Stephenson gained orders for eight locos of the 'Planet' class, and these operated services on the opening day and through the 1830s.

Two views of the new L & M, showing Wapping Tunnel at the Liverpool end of the line, and Chat Moss, a tract of marshy land over which the railway had to pass. Problems of construction over such land were solved by John Dixon, a junior engineer, who filled the peat bog with tree branches, dry turf, hedge cuttings, heather and gravel ballast to form an embankment which carried the line over a distance of 4 miles.

Intersection bridges at St Helens with a 'Planet' class loco in view.

The skew bridge at Rainhill. This was the place where the locomotive trials actually took place. One of Stephenson's locos is at the head of a train and a stagecoach is crossing above the railway. Advent of the passenger railway caused the demise of road coaches in a very short space of time, just as the motor car has done so much damage to the railways in the second half of the twentieth century, although the railway has made something of a comeback.

One of the great engineering features on the L & M was the nine arch Sankey Viaduct which crossed the Manchester Ship Canal. It is seen here with an L & M train making a crossing in the early 1830s.

RAILWAYS IN THE "THIRTIES"

RAILWAY OFFICE, LIVERPOOL.

The Liverpool terminus of the L & M at Crown Street in the 1830s. The station was approached through Wapping Tunnel. This proved to be inadequate even before the construction of the Grand Junction Railway, which had been promoted in 1832 and opened in 1837. Another problem was that the station was sited some distance away from the centre of the city and so first class passengers had to be taken by horse-drawn coach from the station to Dale Street in the city centre. These problems were only solved when, on 23 May 1832, the L & M was authorized to build a tunnel from Edge Hill down to Lime Street, where a new station would be erected before the Grand Junction Railway was opened.

A pair of faded photographs featuring a Webb? 2–4–0 of the LNWR taken by a Mr Adolph Bodenham of Manchester in the 1860s. We think that the pictures were taken at the L & M terminus of Manchester (Liverpool Road). Some special event seems to have brought the photographer here, as all of the station staff and loco crew have been posed for the occasion. We would be very interested to know if there were any special reasons for these pictures.

Lime Street, Liverpool, with St George's Hall on the left and the imposing façade of Lime Street station on the right. The station was built to replace the L & M station at Crown Street and was opened for business on 15 August 1836, a little under a year before Grand Junction Railway services began. Such was the civic pride in the Lime Street project that the town actually contributed £2,000 to enhance the appearance of the station façade. When the station first opened, until March 1870, locos were detached at Edge Hill and trains were worked down the incline by special tunnel brakes accompanied by 'bank riders'. Horses were used to shunt carriages in the station itself.

The exterior of Liverpool Lime Street station when it was under LNWR control. Under the LNWR, Lime Street station was enlarged in 1848, the first of several improvements to be carried out. The final station was provided with eleven platforms, cut back to nine on electrification, and the whole was covered with a twin-arched iron and glass roof, visible on the extreme right of the picture. As this was a terminus station, a concourse was provided between the station frontage and the platforms where passengers could approach the platforms and obtain tickets, and which contained all the station facilities.

THE MERSEYSIDE EXPRESS

LIVERPOOL (Lime Street) and LONDON (Euston)

	Week-days am			Week-days pm
Liverpool (Lime Street) .... dep	10 0		London (Euston) .... dep	6 5
	pm		Mossley Hill .. .. arr	9B48
London (Euston) .. ..arr	IA45		Liverpool (Lime Street) .... ,,	10 6

Restaurant Car Train

A—On Saturdays arrives London (Euston) I 52 pm.   **B**—On Saturdays arrives Mossley Hill 9 52 pm.

Seats on these trains are reservable in advance for passengers travelling from London (Euston), Manchester (London Road), and Liverpool (Lime Street) on payment of fee of I/- per seat.

A timetable for one of the famous expresses that started from Lime Street. 'The Merseyside Express' was usually hauled by 'Princess Royal' Pacifics stabled at Edge Hill locoshed (8A) in LMS and BR steam days, and English-Electric Type 4 diesel-electric locos from the late 1950s until electrification.

The main entrance to Liverpool Lime Street in LNWR days along the shortest street in Liverpool. On the left is a Punch and Judy puppet show, run by one Professor Codman whose family now runs such shows in Llandudno on the North Wales coast. For many years the concourse at Lime Street was the haunt of 'ladies of the night' who hoped to do business with the many sailors arriving at the station to join ships at the famous seaport. Prostitutes would often come to Lime Street station from outside Liverpool, attracted by the number of seamen in the city and, during the Second World War, by soldiers arriving in Liverpool before embarkation to Europe. Business increased when the Americans arrived with their promises of such luxuries as nylon stockings, chocolate and chewing gum. Many of the prostitutes from outside the area were very soon seen off by Liverpool girls who considered Lime Street as their exclusive territory. Even ordinary women, who were on the concourse to meet friends and relatives from trains, were accosted and threatened by prostitutes who thought they were there to take 'business' from them. They would usually be very apologetic when these women proved to be no threat but it must surely have been a very uncomfortable experience for ordinary women at the station.

As improvements to Lime Street station were underway, the approach tunnel from Edge Hill was opened out, as can be seen in this view. The church of St Simon, near the tunnel mouth, was twice taken down and rebuilt. Not until June 1885 was quadrupling of the line from Edge Hill to Lime Street finally completed. Edge Hill was the site of a large goods yard, as well as home to famous locomotives.

LNWR 2–2–2 loco no. 173 *Cornwall*, with 8 ft 6 in driving wheels, was built at Crewe in 1847 and rebuilt in 1858. Between November 1890 and May 1902, the engine was a familiar sight at the head of 40 minute expresses between Liverpool Lime Street and Manchester London Road.

A LNWR three-horse 'brake' coach, which carried railway passengers from Lime Street station to the docks for boats to the Isle of Man.

Manchester London Road station, on the right of this picture, with the Great Central Railway's goods yard on the left. When the GJR was opened in 1837, Liverpool Road station was extended to cope with increasing traffic demands, but an independent line to the Midlands and London was demanded and two schemes were launched: the Manchester & Cheshire Junction Railway planned to build a railway to join the GJR at Crewe, running via Stockport, while the Manchester South Union Railway planned to avoid the GJR altogether, running through the Potteries and joining the Birmingham and Derby Junction Railway at Tamworth, thus giving a direct route, via Rugby, to London. The GJR raised objections and only a line via Stockport to Crewe was built running from a new terminus at Manchester London Road. The new station opened on 8 May 1842 and was built on a viaduct of sixteen arches with a façade, containing all offices in an Italianate style.

THE MANCUNIAN

MANCHESTER (London Road) and LONDON (Euston)

	Week-days am			Week-days pm
Manchester (London Road).......... dep 9 45		London (Euston) .... dep 6 0		
	pm	Wilmslow .. .. arr 9 18		
London (Euston) .. .. .. arr 1 23		Manchester (London Road) .... ,, 9 45		

Restaurant Car Train

A timetable for 'The Mancunian', which ran from Euston to London Road. This train was handled by top-link locos from Longsight shed.

The entrance to Manchester London Road station at the turn of the century. Horse-drawn hansom cabs dominate the scene and people are dressed in the fashions of the day. The arched iron and glass train shed can be seen on the right of the photograph.

An unidentified LNWR 'Precursor' class 4–4–0 heads a train from Euston to Manchester at the turn of the century. These trains were headed by famous locos from the LNWR and LMS over the years; most shedded at Longsight depot.

THE COMET
LONDON (Euston) and MANCHESTER (London Road)

		Mons. to Fris.	Sats. only						Week-days
		am	am						pm
London (Euston) .... dep		9 45	9 35	Manchester (London Road)	....	dep	5· 50		
		pm	pm	Stockport (Edgeley) ..	..	..	„	6 4	
Stoke-on-Trent .. arr		12 34	—	Crewe			„	6 39	
Macclesfield .... „		1 8	—	London (Euston)	..	..	.. arr	9 36	
Stockport (Edgeley).. „		1 28	1 2						
Manchester (Lon. Rd.) „		1 41	1 18						

Restaurant Car Train

A timetable for 'The Comet' which ran from London Road to Euston via Stoke-on-Trent along the North Staffordshire Railway route.

An unidentified English-Electric type 4 (class 40) 1Co-Co1 diesel-electric locomotive at Manchester Longsight depot. The shed, in steam days, provided top-link express locos for trains operating out of Manchester London Road, as its allocation for 30 January 1954 shows:

LMS Code 9A
LMS Stanier 2–6–2T: 40077, 40107, 40136
MR 2P 4–4–0: 40405, 40482, 40539
LMS 2P 4–4–0: 40674, 40693
LMS 4P 4–4–0: 41159, 41168
LMS 2P 0–4–4T: 41905, 41906, 41907
LSM Fowler 2–6–4T: 42308, 42322, 42350, 42351, 42391, 42397, 42398, 42399
LMS Stanier 2–6–4T: 42427, 42430, 42467, 42478, 42542, 42575, 42594, 42599, 42608
LMS Hughes-Fowler 'Crab' 2–6–0: 42772, 42776, 32778, 42814, 42848, 42858, 42886, 42887, 42889, 42923, 42924, 42925, 42930, 42932, 42935, 42936, 42937, 42938
LMS Stanier 2–6–0: 42960
MR 3F 0–6–0: 43275, 43457, 43717
LMS 4F 0–6–0: 44069, 44349, 44357
LMS 'Black Five' 4–6–0: 44686, 44687, 44741, 44742, 44748, 44749, 44750, 44751, 44752, 44760, 44935, 44937, 44941, 45109, 45385
LMS 'Patriot' class 4–6–0: 45500 *Patriot*; 45501 *St Dunstan's*; 45520 *Llandudno*; 45530 *Sir Frank Ree*; 45536 *Private W. Wood VC*; 45539 *E.C. Trench*; 45540 *Sir Robert Turnbull*
LMS 'Jubilee' class 4–6–0: 45553 *Canada*; 45555 *Quebec*; 45556 *Nova Scotia*; 45578 *United Provinces*; 45587 *Baroda*; 45595 *Southern Rhodesia*; 45624 *St Helena*; 45631 *Tanganyika*; 45632 *Tonga*; 45638 *Zanzibar*; 45644 *Howe*; 45680 *Camperdown*; 45689 *Ajax*; 45709 *Implacable*; 45723 *Fearless*
LMS 'Royal Scot' 4–6–0: 46111 *Royal Fusilier*; 46114 *Coldstream Guardsman*; 46115 *Scots Guardsman*; 46120 *Royal Inniskilling Fusilier*; 46122 *Royal Ulster Rifleman*; 46125 *3rd Carabinier*; 46130 *The West Yorkshire Regiment*; 46131 *The Royal Warwickshire Regiment*; 46143 *The South Staffordshire Regiment*; 46160 *Queen Victoria's Rifleman*; 46161 *King's Own*; 46169 *The Boy Scout*
LMS 'Jinty' 0–6–0T: 47267, 47341, 47343, 47345, 47347, 47369, 47395, 47400, 47528, 47673
LMS 8F 2–8–0: 48389, 48425, 48428, 48500, 48501, 48516, 48633, 48731, 48744
LNWR 7F 0–8–0: 49428, 49439
BR 7P 4–6–2: 70031 *Byron*; 70032 *Tennyson*; 70033 *Charles Dickens*; 70043 *Lord Kitchener*; 70044 *Earl Haig*
BR Class 4 2–6–4T: 80039
Total: 131

The centenary of the L & M was celebrated in September 1930, with one of that company's locos, 0–4–2 *Lion*, still in running order and able to appear with a rake of replica coaches at the event. The engine was built in 1838 by Todd, Kitson and Laird of Leeds for the L & M. As it turned out, by great good fortune, *Lion* was sold to the Mersey Docks and Harbour Board in 1859 for use as a shunting engine. Several years later, the Board made use of her as a stationary engine and she lasted in this form until 1920 when the LMS purchased her for restoration. After appearing in the L & M centenary celebrations, she went to a musuem in Liverpool. *Lion* became a famous film star in 1950 when she appeared in the Ealing comedy *The Titfield Thunderbolt*, a story about people wanting to save a rural branch line for preservation. Although such a thing would have seemed a rather fantastic notion then, history has shown that such things actually did occur.

In 1980, the 150th anniversary of the L & M was celebrated, and a great collection of preserved steam locos appeared at the event. These engines, saved from scrapyards in the 1960s when BR abandoned steam traction from its network, gathered in Manchester and included *Lion* once again. The loco, seen here at Manchester, was still in working order and took part in the cavalcade as the oldest working loco in the world.

Also represented at the 150th anniversary of the L & M were replicas of the original locos involved in the Rainhill Trials. Here, *Sans Pareil* is seen at Liverpool Road awaiting its turn in the cavalcade.

Ex-LMS Stanier 'Black Five' 4–6–0 no. 5407 waits at Manchester Liverpool Road to join the cavalcade. These engines were a familiar sight in Lancashire at the head of passenger and freight trains all over the LMS network.

Ex-LMS 'Royal Scot' class 4–6–0 no. 6115 *Scots Guardsman* at Manchester during the L & M 150th anniversary celebrations. This loco was once shedded at Longsight shed and headed express trains from Manchester to Euston, Birmingham (New Street) and the North Wales coast in steam days.

Preserved ex-Midland Railway 'Compound' 4–4–0 no. 1000, as that company's representative at the L & M celebrations.

Rear view of 1000 at Manchester. These engines appeared in the area under LMS auspices.

OTHER LNWR LOCATIONS

As well as control of the L & M and GJR, the LNWR had considerable influence within Lancashire. The West Coast Main Line runs for a considerable length within the county, passing through towns like Wigan, Preston and Lancaster. The company also had local lines between Liverpool, Manchester and Crewe, along with routes to Bolton, Oldham and the Yorkshire border. The company had major stations, besides Lime Street and London Road, at Liverpool Riverside and Manchester Exchange, along with small wayside stations on its routes to Crewe and the north. These routes and stations saw a great variety of locomotives, from 'top-link' LMS Pacifics to freight engines, and tank locos on local trains. These engines were housed in locosheds, large and small, up and down the county.

The concourse at Liverpool Riverside station, opened on 12 June 1895 by the Mersey Docks & Harbour Board to serve the adjoining Princes Landing Stage. Only a month later, LNWR directors lunched in the baggage room while they watched the unloading of White Star liner *Majestic*. Passengers boarded trains made up of special coaches which had been set aside for such duties, providing a direct service between Liverpool Riverside and Euston. A branch from Edge Hill to Waterloo Goods was used by these trains, while the link to Riverside completed over metals belonging to the Mersey Dock & Harbour Board. Not long after the LMS came into existence, Cunard and White Star Lines announced that Southampton was to become their chief port, with Liverpool taking a secondary role. Despite this the station could still be busy. Indeed, one weekend in August 1924, nine liners were served by seven special trains. Up until 1938, as many as seventy liners were still sailing from Liverpool. The Second World War saw troops arrive and depart in large numbers, first Free French soldiers and later Canadians and Americans. The station was always kept in spotless condition, usually with hanging baskets and potted plants at the buffer end.

Until 27 March 1950, trains were operated by ex-LNWR 0–6–2 'Coal Tanks', occasionally helped out by G2 0–8–0s. Strengthening of the bridge over Princes Dock allowed big engines to journey through the tunnels to Edge Hill and 'Jubilee' class 4–6–0 no. 45567 *South Australia* headed the first boat train to be hauled by a single engine all the way to Euston. The station finally closed on 25 February 1971, a class 40 diesel hauling the last train full of soldiers from Northern Ireland out of the station, eighty-five years after the first train had been run to connect with liner *Germanic*.

Entrance, left, to the LNWR station of Manchester Exchange. This station came into existence as a result of the Lancashire & Yorkshire Railway's refusal to share ownership of their Victoria station, which was at the east end of Exchange. The LNWR transferred its passenger services to Exchange from Victoria on 30 June 1884. Among trains affected were some introduced in March 1882 between Stockport and Victoria, for the convenience of passengers who had formerly had to make their way across Manchester from London Road station to catch LYR trains. With the opening of Exchange station these same passengers were now forced to walk a quarter of a mile or more between Exchange and Victoria. Although this did not involve leaving railway premises, the way through the older part of the station was very inconvenient. The long through platform connecting the two stations was not completed until the 1920s, after the two companies had amalgamated.

Manchester Exchange station, with the Cromwell Monument in front, at the turn of the century. Exchange station was actually in Salford, although the local population regarded it as being in Manchester. The station was approached by means of a wide bridge across the River Irwell. The offices at the front of the station were destroyed during the blitz in the Second World War. On the left of the picture is a travel agency belonging to Thomas Cook & Son, which became famous in the early 1840s for railway excursions. Thomas Cook organized his first one on 5 July 1841 for 1,000 temperance reformers from Leicester to Loughborough. From that time on, his travel agencies spread all over England and were often located close to important railway stations.

Another view of the Cromwell Memorial outside Manchester Exchange station. The statue was the first dedicated to him in Britain and was given to the city in 1875. It is now located in Wythenshawe Park.

Exchange station at the turn of the century. On the right is an LNWR advertisement for excursions to Ireland, then still part of the United Kingdom. Trains ran along the North Wales coast to Holyhead for the sea crossing to Dublin. The railway company is keen to emphasize the beauty of the Welsh coast and the short sea crossing to Ireland. At the end of the station drive there are adverts for a local theatre showing *The Sunshine Girl*.

The interior of Manchester Exchange station, showing the concourse and passenger footbridge as it appeared in LNWR days. Station staff look smart in railway company uniform, while passengers at the booking office are resplendent in top hats and black coats. W.H. Smith has its bookstall on the station, as in a good many other locations, and train destination boards display which trains are to depart at 12.05 p.m. The station was opened in 1884 and closed in the 1970s, although the long through platform between Exchange and Victoria is still in use, serving through trains between Yorkshire and Chester.

LMS Stanier three-cylinder 4–6–0 'Jubilee' class no. 5650, later to be named *Blake*, at the head of a Holyhead-bound parcels train waiting to depart from Exchange station on 4 April 1936.

LNWR Ramsbottom 2–2–2 'Problem' or 'Lady-of-the-Lake' class 2–2–2 no. 60 *Tantalus* at the head of a train in the late nineteenth century. These engines were a fairly common sight in the Manchester area at this time, although they were usually reserved for operating 'Irish Mail' services between Euston and Holyhead.

A 'Trans-Pennine' Diesel Multiple Unit set arrives at Manchester Exchange station from Leeds in 1968. These DMU sets were specially built for passenger services over the Pennines from Manchester Exchange to Leeds, and their modern fronts make them look similar to Electric Multiple Units which operate local services on the 25kv WCML. These DMUs were not a great success and all had disappeared by the mid-1980s, becoming as much a part of history as Exchange station itself.

Worsley station on the LNWR line from Bolton to Eccles, with a local train, hauled by a 2–4–2 tank loco, at the platform. Note the enamel advertisements fixed to the station fences. 'Lipton's Tea' and 'Pears Soap' are most prominent in this view. The line was a branch from the Liverpool and Manchester Railway which terminated at Bolton (Great Moor Street).

Acton Bridge station of the LNWR. The station was on the Grand Junction Railway, between Crewe and Warrington. It was originally named 'Acton', until 1 July 1870, and was rebuilt in 1925 as part of the Crewe–Weaver Junction widening scheme.

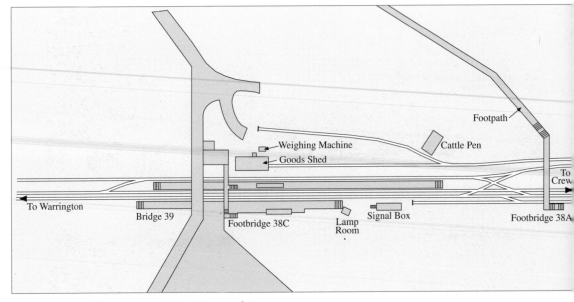

Acton Bridge station, c. 1930. (Not to scale)

Another view of Acton Bridge station. This appears to be the original station prior to rebuilding. The station was fully closed on 4 January 1965.

The LNWR station at Prestbury towards the end of the nineteenth century.

The entrance to the joint station at Stalybridge, its owners being the LNWR and GCR. The LYR also had interests in the town.

Interior of Stalybridge station, looking west, with the no. 3 signalbox straddling the line.

LNWR 'Claughton' class 4–6–0 no. 2221 *Sir Francis Dent* prepares to leave Stalybridge station with a Liverpool–Newcastle express. The first company to arrive in Stalybridge was the Sheffield, Ashton-under-Lyne, & Manchester Railway on 23 December 1845 when its 2¼ mile line from Guide Bridge to Ashton was opened. It became the Manchester, Sheffield & Lincolnshire Railway from 1 January 1847, and part of the Great Central Railway from 1907. A year after opening, Stalybridge became a station on the LNWR and LYR route from Leeds to Manchester. After the 'Grouping', the LMS and LNER shared control of Stalybridge, following arrangements made at the turn of the century, each taking five year turns in office. Unusually, in the 1980s, 'Sprinter' trains from the North Wales coast terminated here, having run through to Hull prior to this. By the early 1990s, these trains terminated at Manchester Victoria or Oxford Road.

Diggle station, on the LNWR main line between Manchester and Leeds, with the portals of Standedge tunnel beyond, and the Pennine range in the distance. The station is included here because it was transferred from the Urban District of Saddleworth (in the West Riding of Yorkshire) to Greater Manchester Metropolitan County in the Local Government reorganization of 1974. In 1845, the Huddersfield & Manchester Railway received Royal Assent to build a line through Standedge, the tunnel finally opening in 1849 allowing the line to begin operations. By this time, the H & MR had become part of the mighty LNWR. The single-bore tunnel soon became a bottleneck as traffic through Diggle expanded rapidly, but it took twenty years before a new tunnel was constructed. This new Standedge tunnel was opened for traffic on 24 April 1871. The railway and tunnels remain open today, but Diggle station closed on 5 October 1968.

Ex-LMS Stanier 8F 2–8–0 no. 48695 close to the coaling plant at Carnforth shed on 15 May 1964. The shed provided local passenger and freight locos for traffic in the Lancaster area. Coded 11A, its allocation for 30 January 1954 was as follows:

LMS Fowler 2–6–2T: 40011, 40041, 40070
LMS Stanier 2–6–4T: 42428, 42429, 42432, 42544, 42573, 42601
LMS 4F 0–6–0: 44192, 44306, 44399, 44510
LMS 'Black Five' 4–6–0: 44709, 44874, 44892, 44904, 44905, 45017, 45019, 45054, 45072, 45092, 45133, 45193, 45241, 45306, 45326, 45327, 45392, 45427
LMS 'Jinty' 3F 0–6–0T: 47317, 47339, 47406, 47409, 47410, 47605
LNWR 'Super D' 0–8–0: 49109, 49130, 49144, 49252, 49438, 49439
Total: 43

Ex-LMS Stanier 2–6–4 tank loco no. 42449 rests at the entrance to Carnforth locoshed on 15 May 1964.

The locoshed at Carnforth was closed by BR on 6 September 1965, but was purchased two years later as a base for a steam railway museum. When private steam locomotive-hauled railtours returned to the BR main line in the 1970s, Carnforth shed became a centre for such trains, having adopted the title of 'Steamtown'. Here, on 19 August 1985, one of Steamtown's collection of engines, ex-LYR Aspinall 0–6–0 no. 1300 (ex BR no. 52322), stands outside the old locoshed.

THE LANCASHIRE & YORKSHIRE RAILWAY

Beginning as the Manchester & Leeds Railway, it opened on 1 March 1841 after several unsuccessful attempts to gain parliamentary approval in the 1830s. The M & L finally received Royal Assent on 4 July 1837, after its prospectus pointed out that the proposed line would run through centres of high population. The name was changed to the Lancashire & Yorkshire Railway in 1848 when it amalgamated with the Liverpool & Bury Railway, thus giving the company access to Liverpool via Bolton. The M & L ran from Manchester Victoria station, which in 1846 claimed to be the largest station in England, to Normanton, where it joined the North Midland Railway for access to Leeds. The line gave Manchester and the Lancashire towns on the route a link with Derby, Nottingham and Leicester, as well as a round about route to London.

Back in Liverpool, the LYR went on to establish a station at Exchange, which it shared with the East Lancashire Railway, the two becoming bitter rivals until the ELR was absorbed into the LYR in 1859. The ELR grew up around Bury when the Manchester, Bury & Rossendale Railway proposed a scheme in 1844 to leave the Manchester and Bolton line at Clifton and pass through Bury and Rawtenstall (a manufacturing village in the Irwell Valley). The M & L proposed a scheme for extension to Bury, but the MB & R won parliamentary approval because its proposals went beyond Bury to other districts. Thus, the MB & R won its Act on 4 July 1844, becoming part of the ELR on 21 July 1845, and its line opened on 28 September 1846. The ELR also absorbed the line which served Blackburn, Burnley, Accrington and Colne.

The LYR had a line to Southport by absorption of the near bankrupt West Lancashire Railway under an Act of 15 July 1897. The company also had a line to Blackpool through joint control with the LNWR of the Preston & Wyre Railway which had absorbed the Blackpool and Lytham Railway in 1871.

At the turn of the century, the LYR ventured into electrification of its suburban network around Liverpool, work on the line to Southport being completed in 1904. By July 1906 electric trains ran to Aintree, to Maghull in 1909, to Aughton in 1911 and to Ormskirk in 1913. Also, in 1913, electric trains ran in the Bury area.

The LYR had its own locomotive construction works in Lancashire, at Horwich near Wigan. The works covered 116 acres, of which over 22 were occupied by the buildings, including the 1,520 ft long erecting shop. The works was begun by Aspinall, the CME, in 1886, and the first loco was completed there in 1889. This was a 2–4–2 radial tank, the first of a class that eventually numbered 270.

The LYR ceased to exist in 1922 when it amalgamated with the LNWR, a company that was always friendly, in anticipation of the 1923 'Grouping' when they became part of the new LMS. Ex-LYR Chief Mechanical Engineer at Horwich, George Hughes, became the first CME of the LMS in 1923, thus perpetuating LYR influence for three more years until replaced by Henry Fowler.

Ex-LMS Stanier 8F no. 48026 stands beyond the north end of platforms 12 and 13 at the old LYR's Manchester Victoria station in 1968. On the far right, a DMU is departing with a train for Chester and the North Wales coast. This picture would have been taken only a few weeks before steam finally disappeared from the BR network, as Lancashire was the last county in Britain to see steam-hauled trains.

Table 143	MANCHESTER, BOLTON, BLACKBURN AND HELLIFIELD

WEEKDAYS

Manchester (Victoria) ....dep	
Salford	
Bolton (Trinity Street)............	
The Oaks..........................	
Bromley Cross	
Turton and Edgworth..............	
Entwistle	
Spring Vale	
Darwen	
Lower Darwen	
Blackburn......................arr	
153 Liverpool (Exchange)..........dep	
Blackburn.......................dep	
Daisy Field	
Wilpshire (for Ribchester)........	
Langho	
Whalley	
Clitheroe.........................	
Chatburn	
Rimington	
Gisburn..........................	
Newsholme.......................	
Hellifield.......................arr	
Ingleton ....arr	
181 Morecambe (Promenade)........	
Carnforth	
Carlisle	

A 1950s timetable for passenger trains operating over the old LYR route from Manchester Victoria to Hellifield, via Bolton and Blackburn.

Manchester Victoria station in the 1970s, with a DMU approaching the station with a local train and a class 40 hauled express on the right. When the station opened in 1846, it was claimed to be the largest in England, but all business was conducted at only one very long platform, the east end of which was for Leeds trains and the west for Liverpool-bound services. All other tracks were connected to the platform by turntables.

Manchester Victoria in the early 1980s. The roof was originally an iron and glass structure supported by north and south walls and rows of columns. The long, single-storey main building was described as in 'Roman Doric' style.

The west end of Victoria station in the 1970s. Back in 1847 some fifty-eight trains were booked to leave the station daily. By 1882 this number had increased to 258, making the station very busy indeed.

Nowadays steam traction is regarded as the extinct method of propulsion but it is easy to forget that many of the old diesels which ousted steam locomotives have themselves disappeared from the railway scene. One such type is the old class 40 diesel-electric, common on the Lancashire system and beyond, an example of which, no. 40091, is seen here at Victoria station in the 1970s.

Table 146

MANCHESTER AND BURY

WEEKDAYS

Mls.		a.m.	a.m.	a.m.	a.m.	a.m.	a.m.	a.m.	a.m.	a.m.	SX a.m.	a.m.	a.m.
0	**Manchester** (Victoria) dep	5 15	5 25	5 50	6 10	6 30	6 50	7 9	7 20	7 30	7 37	7 48	7 57
2	Woodlands Road	Steam Train	5 29	5 54	6 14	6 34	6 54	7 13	7 24	7 34	...	7 52	...
2¼	Crumpsall		5 31	5 56	6 16	6 36	6 56	7 15	7 26	7 36	7 43	7 54	8 2
3¼	Bowker Vale		5 33	5 58	6 18	6 38	6 58	7 17	7 28	7 38	7 45	7 56	8 4
4	Heaton Park		5 35	6 0	6 20	6 40	7 0	7 19	7 30	7 40	7 47	7 58	8 6
4¼	Prestwich		5 37	6 2	6 22	6 42	7 2	7 21	7 32	7 42	7 49	8 0	8 8
5¼	Besses-o'th'-Barn		5 39	6 4	6 24	6 44	7 4	7 23	7 34	7 44	7 51	8 2	8 10
6	Whitefield		5 41	6 6	6 26	6 46	7 6	7 25	7 36	7 46	7 53	8 4	8 12
7½	Radcliffe (Central)	5 32	5 44	6 9	6 29	6 49	7 9	7 28	7 39	7 49	7 56	8 7	8 15
9½	**Bury** (Bolton Street) arr	5 38	5 49	6 14	6 34	6 54	7 14	7 33	...	7 54	8 1	8 12	8 22
	145 Bacup arr	6 37	.	.	7 25	.	.	.	.	.	.	8 55	.

	a.m.	a.m.	a.m.	a.m.	a.m.	a.m.	a.m.	a.m.	a.m.	a.m.	a.m.	
Manchester (Victoria) dep	8 8	8 30	8 39	8 42	8 51	9 0	9 10	9 40	10 10	10 40	11 10	.
Woodlands Road	8 12	8 34	...	8 46	8 55	9 4	9 14	9 44	10 14	10 44	11 14	...
Crumpsall	8 14	8 36	8 44	8 48	8 57	9 6	9 16	9 46	10 16	10 46	11 16	.
Bowker Vale	8 16	8 38	8 46	8 50	8 59	9 8	9 18	9 48	10 18	10 48	11 18	...
Heaton Park	8 18	8 40	8 48	8 52	9 1	9 10	9 20	9 50	10 20	10 50	11 20	.
Prestwich	8 20	8 42	8 50	8 54	9 3	9 12	9 22	9 52	10 22	10 52	11 22	...
Besses-o'th'-Barn	8 22	8 44	.	8 56	9 5	9 14	9 24	9 54	10 24	10 54	11 24	.
Whitefield	8 24	8 46	...	8 58	9 7	9 16	9 26	9 56	10 26	10 56	11 26	...
Radcliffe (Central)	8 27	8 49	.	9 3	9 11	9 19	9 29	9 59	10 29	10 59	11 29	.
Bury (Bolton Street) arr	8 32	8 54	...	9 9	9 17	9 24	9 34	10 4	10 34	11 4	11 34	...
145 Bacup arr	.	.	.	9 49	.	.	.	10*49	.	.	.	.

	a.m.	noon	SO p.m.	SO p.m.	p.m.	SO p.m.		SO p.m.	p.m.	SO p.m.	SO p.m.
Manchester (Victoria) dep	11 40	12 0	12 7	12 10	12 15	12 20	.	12 25	12 30	12 36	12 40
Woodlands Road	11 44	12 4	...	12 14	12 19	12 24	...	...	12 34	...	12 44
Crumpsall	11 46	12 6	12 12	12 16	12 21	12 26	.	12 30	12 36	12 41	12 46
Bowker Vale	11 48	12 8	12 14	12 18	12 23	12 28	...	...	12 38	12 43	12 48
Heaton Park	11 50	12 10	12 16	12 20	12 25	12 30	.	12 33	12 40	12 45	12 50
Prestwich	11 52	12 12	12 18	12 22	12 27	12 32	...	12 35	12 42	12 47	12 52
Besses-o'th'-Barn	11 54	12 14	.	12 24	12 29	12 34	.	.	12 44	.	12 54
Whitefield	11 56	12 16	...	12 26	12 31	12 36	...	...	12 46	...	12 56
Radcliffe (Central)	11 59	12 19	.	12 29	12 34	12 39	.	.	12 49	.	1 0
Bury (Bolton Street) arr	12 4	12 24	...	12 34	12 39	12 44	...	...	12 54	...	1 5
145 Bacup arr	12*44	.	.	.	1 18	.	.	.	.	.	.

WEEKDAYS — continued.

	SO p.m.		p.m.	SO p.m.	SX p.m.		SO p.m.	p.m.	SO p.m.	p.m.		p.m.
Manchester (Victoria) dep	12 50	.	1 0	1 13	1 15	.	1 20	1 30	1 40	1 50	.	2 10
Woodlands Road	12 54	...	1 4	1 17	1 19	...	1 24	1 34	1 44	1 54	...	2 14
Crumpsall	12 56	.	1 6	1 19	1 21	.	1 26	1 36	1 46	1 56	.	2 16
Bowker Vale	12 58	...	1 8	1 21	1 23	...	1 28	1 38	1 48	1 58	...	2 18
Heaton Park	1 0	.	1 10	1 23	1 25	.	1 30	1 40	1 50	2 0	.	2 20
Prestwich	1 2	...	1 12	1 25	1 27	...	1 32	1 42	1 52	2 2	...	2 22
Besses-o'th'-Barn	1 4	.	1 14	1 27	1 29	.	1 34	1 44	1 54	2 4	.	2 24
Whitefield	1 6	...	1 16	1 29	1 31	...	1 36	1 46	1 56	2 6	...	2 26
Radcliffe (Central)	1 9	.	1 19	1 32	1 34	.	1 39	1 49	1 59	2 9	.	2 29
Bury (Bolton Street) arr	1 14	...	1 24	1 37	1 39	...	1 44	1 54	2 4	2 14	...	2 34
145 Bacup arr	.	.	.	.	.	.	.	2SO24	.	2SX59	.	.

	SO p.m.		SX p.m.	SO p.m.	p.m.	SO p.m.	SX p.m.	SO p.m.	p.m.	p.m.	SX p.m.	p.m.
Manchester (Victoria) dep	2 30	.	2 40	2 50	3 10	3 30	3 40	3 50	4 10	4 30	4 40	4 50
Woodlands Road	2 34	...	2 44	2 54	3 14	3 34	3 44	3 54	4 14	4 34	4 44	4 54
Crumpsall	2 36	.	2 46	2 56	3 16	3 36	3 46	3 56	4 16	4 36	4 46	4 56
Bowker Vale	2 38	...	2 48	2 58	3 18	3 38	3 48	3 58	4 18	4 38	4 48	4 58
Heaton Park	2 40	.	2 50	3 0	3 20	3 40	3 50	4 0	4 20	4 40	4 50	5 0
Prestwich	2 42	...	2 52	3 2	3 22	3 42	3 52	4 2	4 22	4 42	4 52	5 2
Besses-o'th'-Barn	2 44	.	2 54	3 4	3 24	3 44	3 54	4 4	4 24	4 44	4 54	5 4
Whitefield	2 46	...	2 56	3 6	3 26	3 46	3 56	4 6	4 26	4 46	4 56	5 6
Radcliffe (Central)	2 49	.	2 59	3 9	3 29	3 49	3 59	4 9	4 29	4 49	4 59	5 9
Bury (Bolton Street) arr	2 54	...	3 4	3 14	3 34	3 54	4 4	4 14	4 34	4 54	5 4	5 14
145 Bacup arr	3 38	.	.	.	.	4 47	4 47	.	.	5 37	6 2	.

	SX p.m.	SX p.m.	p.m.		SX p.m.	SX p.m.	SX p.m.	p.m.		SX p.m.	SX p.m.
Manchester (Victoria) dep	5 0	5 5	5 10	.	5 15	5 20	5 24	5 30	.	5 37	5 40
Woodlands Road	5 4	5 9	5 14	...	5 19	5 24	5 28	5 34	...	...	5 44
Crumpsall	5 6	5 11	5 16	.	5 21	5 26	5 30	5 36	.	5 42	5 46
Bowker Vale	5 8	5 13	5 18	...	5 23	5 28	...	5 38	...	...	5 48
Heaton Park	5 10	5 15	5 20	.	5 25	5 30	5 33	5 40	.	5 45	5 50
Prestwich	5 12	5 17	5 23	...	5 27	5 32	5 35	5 42	...	5 47	5 52
Besses-o'th'-Barn	5 14	.	5 25	.	5 29	5 34	.	5 44	.	5 49	5 54
Whitefield	5 16	...	5 27	...	5 31	5 36	...	5 46	...	5 51	5 56
Radcliffe (Central)	5 19	...	5 30	...	5 34	5 39	.	5 49	.	5 54	5 59
Bury (Bolton Street) arr	5 24	...	5 35	...	...	5 44	...	5 54	...	...	6 4
145 Bacup arr	.	.	6SO15	.	.	6 24	.	.	.	.	.

WEEKDAYS — continued.

	SO p.m.	SX p.m.	SX p.m.	p.m.	SX p.m.	p.m.	SX p.m.	SO p.m.	SX p.m.	p.m.	SO p.m.	SX p.m.
Manchester (Victoria) dep	5 50	5 55	6 0	6 10	6 20	6 30	6 40	6 50	6 55	7 10	7 30	7 40
Woodlands Road	5 54	5 59	6 4	6 14	6 24	6 34	6 44	6 54	6 59	7 14	7 34	7 44
Crumpsall	5 56	6 1	6 6	6 16	6 26	6 36	6 46	6 56	7 1	7 16	7 36	7 46
Bowker Vale	5 58	6 3	6 8	6 18	6 28	6 38	6 48	6 58	7 3	7 18	7 38	7 48
Heaton Park	6 0	6 5	6 10	6 20	6 30	6 40	6 50	7 0	7 5	7 20	7 40	7 50
Prestwich	6 2	6 7	6 12	6 22	6 32	6 42	6 52	7 2	7 7	7 22	7 42	7 52
Besses-o'th'-Barn	6 4	6 9	6 14	6 24	6 34	6 44	6 54	7 4	7 9	7 24	7 44	7 54
Whitefield	6 6	6 11	6 16	6 26	6 36	6 46	6 56	7 6	7 11	7 26	7 46	7 56
Radcliffe (Central)	6 9	6 14	6 19	6 29	6 39	6 49	6 59	7 10	7 14	7 29	7 49	7 59
Bury (Bolton Street) arr	6 14	6 19	6 24	6 34	6 44	6 54	7 4	7 15	7 19	7 34	7 54	8 4
Bacup arr	.	7 3	.	7SO29	7 29	.	.	.	.	8 18	.	8 57

	SO p.m.	p.m.	SO p.m.	SX p.m.	SO p.m.	p.m.	SO p.m.	SX p.m.	SO p.m.	p.m.	
Manchester (Victoria) dep	7 50	8 10	8 30	8 40	8 50	9 10	9 30	9 40	9 50	10 10	.
Woodlands Road	7 54	8 14	8 34	8 44	8 54	9 14	9 34	9 44	9 54	10 14	...
Crumpsall	7 56	8 16	8 36	8 46	8 56	9 16	9 36	9 46	9 56	10 16	.
Bowker Vale	7 58	8 18	8 38	8 48	8 58	9 18	9 38	9 48	9 58	10 18	...
Heaton Park	8 0	8 20	8 40	8 50	9 0	9 20	9 40	9 50	10 0	10 20	.
Prestwich	8 2	8 22	8 42	8 52	9 2	9 22	9 42	9 52	10 2	10 22	...
Besses-o'th'-Barn	8 4	8 24	8 44	8 54	9 4	9 24	9 44	9 54	10 4	10 24	.
Whitefield	8 6	8 26	8 46	8 56	9 6	9 26	9 46	9 56	10 6	10 26	...
Radcliffe (Central)	8 9	8 29	8 49	8 59	9 9	9 29	9 49	9 59	10 9	10 29	.
Bury (Bolton Street) arr	8 14	8 34	8 54	9 4	9 14	9 34	9 54	10 4	10 14	10 34	...
Bacup arr	8 57	.	.	9 49	9 57	.	10 46	10 46	.	11SO17	.

	SO p.m.	SX p.m.	SO p.m.	SO p.m.	SX p.m.	SO p.m.	p.m.
Manchester (Victoria) dep	10 30	10 40	10 50	11 0	11 10	11 20	11 37
Woodlands Road	10 34	10 44	10 54	11 4	11 14	11 24	11 41
Crumpsall	10 36	10 46	10 56	11 6	11 16	11 26	11 43
Bowker Vale	10 38	10 48	10 58	11 8	11 18	11 28	11 45
Heaton Park	10 40	10 50	11 0	11 10	11 20	11 30	11 47
Prestwich	10 42	10 52	11 2	11 12	11 22	11 32	11 49
Besses-o'th'-Barn	10 44	10 54	11 4	11 14	11 24	11 34	11 51
Whitefield	10 46	10 56	11 6	11 16	11 26	11 36	11 53
Radcliffe (Central)	10 49	10 59	11 9	11 19	11 29	11 39	11 56
Bury (Bolton Street) arr	10 54	11 4	11 14	11 24	11 34	11 44	12 1
Bacup arr	.	11 42	12 0	.	.	.	.

✱—Third class only. SO—Saturdays only. SX—Saturdays excepted.

Table 146
continued.

MANCHESTER AND BURY

SUNDAYS

	a.m.	a.m.	a.m.	a.m.	a.m.	a.m.	a.m.	a.m.	a.m.	a.m.	p.m.	p.m.
Manchester (Victoria) dep	6 45	7 40	8 15	8 50	9 20	9 50	10 20	10 50	11 20	11 50	12 20	12 50
Woodlands Road	6 49	7 44	8 19	8 54	9 24	9 54	10 24	10 54	11 24	11 54	12 24	12 54
Crumpsall	6 51	7 46	8 21	8 56	9 26	9 56	10 26	10 56	11 26	11 56	12 26	12 56
Bowker Vale	6 53	7 48	8 23	8 58	9 28	9 58	10 28	10 58	11 28	11 58	12 28	12 58
Heaton Park	6 55	7 50	8 25	9 0	9 30	10 0	10 30	11 0	11 30	12 0	12 30	1 0
Prestwich	6 57	7 52	8 27	9 2	9 32	10 2	10 32	11 2	11 32	12 2	12 32	1 2
Besses-o'th'-Barn	6 59	7 54	8 29	9 4	9 34	10 4	10 34	11 4	11 34	12 4	12 34	1 4
Whitefield	7 1	7 56	8 31	9 6	9 36	10 6	10 36	11 6	11 36	12 6	12 36	1 6
Radcliffe (Central)	7 4	7 59	8 34	9 9	9 39	10 9	10 39	11 9	11 39	12 9	12 39	1 9
Bury (Bolton Street) arr	7 9	8 4	8 39	9 14	9 44	10 14	10 44	11 14	11 44	12 14	12 44	1 14
Bacup arr	.	.	.	.	.	.	.	11 55	.	.	.	.

	p.m.	p.m.	p.m.	p.m.	p.m.	p.m.	p.m.	p.m.	p.m.	p.m.	p.m.	p.m.
Manchester (Victoria) dep	1 20	1 50	2 20	2 50	3 20	3 50	4 20	4 50	5 20	5 50	6 20	6 50
Woodlands Road	1 24	1 54	2 24	2 54	3 24	3 54	4 24	4 54	5 24	5 54	6 24	6 54
Crumpsall	1 26	1 56	2 26	2 56	3 26	3 56	4 26	4 56	5 26	5 56	6 26	6 56
Bowker Vale	1 28	1 58	2 28	2 58	3 28	3 58	4 28	4 58	5 28	5 58	6 28	6 58
Heaton Park	1 30	2 0	2 30	3 0	3 30	4 0	4 30	5 0	5 30	6 0	6 30	7 0
Prestwich	1 32	2 2	2 32	3 2	3 32	4 2	4 32	5 2	5 32	6 2	6 32	7 2
Besses-o'th'-Barn	1 34	2 4	2 34	3 4	3 34	4 4	4 34	5 4	5 34	6 4	6 34	7 4
Whitefield	1 36	2 6	2 36	3 6	3 36	4 6	4 36	5 6	5 36	6 6	6 36	7 6
Radcliffe (Central)	1 39	2 9	2 39	3 9	3 39	4 9	4 39	5 9	5 39	6 9	6 39	7 9
Bury (Bolton Street) arr	1 44	2 14	2 44	3 14	3 44	4 14	4 44	5 14	5 44	6 14	6 44	7 14
Bacup arr	.	.	.	4 5	.	.	.	.	6 27	.	.	.

	p.m.	p.m.	p.m.		p.m.	p.m.	p.m.	p.m.	p.m.	p.m.
Manchester (Victoria) dep	7 20	7 50	8 20	.	8 50	9 20	9 50	10 20	10 40	11 10
Woodlands Road	7 24	7 54	8 24	...	8 54	9 24	9 54	10 24	10 44	11 14
Crumpsall	7 26	7 56	8 26	.	8 56	9 26	9 56	10 26	10 46	11 16
Bowker Vale	7 28	7 58	8 28	...	8 58	9 28	9 58	10 28	10 48	11 18
Heaton Park	7 30	8 0	8 30	.	9 0	9 30	10 0	10 30	10 50	11 20
Prestwich	7 32	8 2	8 32	...	9 2	9 32	10 2	10 32	10 52	11 22
Besses-o'th'-Barn	7 34	8 4	8 34	.	9 4	9 34	10 4	10 34	10 54	11 24
Whitefield	7 36	8 6	8 36	...	9 6	9 36	10 6	10 36	10 56	11 26
Radcliffe (Central)	7 39	8 9	8 39	.	9 9	9 39	10 9	10 39	10 59	11 29
Bury (Bolton Street) arr	7 44	8 14	8 44	...	9 14	9 44	10 14	10 44	11 4	11 34
Bacup arr	.	8 55	.	.	.	10 29	.	.	.	.

WEEKDAYS

Mls.		a.m.	a.m.	a.m.	a.m.	a.m.		a.m.	SX a.m.	a.m.	a.m.	SX a.m.	SO a.m.
	145 Bacup dep	.	.	5 24	.	.	.	.	.	.	.	6 58	6 58
0	**Bury** (Bolton Street) dep	5 20	5 40	6 0	6 20	6 40	...	7 0	7 10	7 20	7 30	7 37	7 40
2¼	Radcliffe (Central) "	5 24	5 44	6 4	6 24	6 44	.	7 4	7 14	7 24	7 34	7 41	7 44
3½	Whitefield	5 27	5 47	6 7	6 27	6 47	...	7 7	7 17	7 27	7 37	7 44	7 47
4¼	Besses-o'th'-Barn	5 29	5 49	6 9	6 29	6 49	.	7 9	7 19	7 29	7 39	7 46	7 49
5¼	Prestwich	5 30	5 50	6 10	6 30	6 50	...	7 10	7 20	7 30	7 40	7 47	7 50
5¾	Heaton Park	5 32	5 52	6 12	6 32	6 52	.	7 12	7 22	7 32	7 42	7 49	7 52
6¼	Bowker Vale	5 34	5 54	6 14	6 34	6 54	...	7 14	7 24	7 34	7 44	7 51	7 54
7¼	Crumpsall	5 36	5 56	6 16	6 36	6 56	.	7 16	7 26	7 36	7 46	7 53	7 56
7¾	Woodlands Road	5 38	5 58	6 18	6 38	6 58	...	7 18	7 28	7 38	7 48	7 55	7 58
9¼	**Manchester** (Victoria) arr	5 43	6 3	6 23	6 43	7 3	.	7 23	7 33	7 43	7 53	8 0	8 3

	SX a.m.	a.m.	a.m.	a.m.	a.m.	a.m.	SX a.m.	SO a.m.	a.m.	a.m.	a.m.	a.m.
145 Bacup dep	.	.	.	.	.	.	.	.	7 40	.	.	.
Bury (Bolton Street) dep	7 43	7 50	...	8 0	...	8 9	...	...	8 20	...	8 30	8 35
Radcliffe (Central) "	7 47	7 54	7 59	8 4	8 9	8 13	.	8 17	8 24	.	8 34	8 39
Whitefield	7 50	7 57	8 2	8 7	8 12	8 16	8 22	8 22	8 27	...	8 37	8 42
Besses-o'th'-Barn	7 52	7 59	8 4	8 9	8 14	8 18	8 24	8 24	8 29	.	8 39	8 44
Prestwich	7 53	8 0	8 5	8 10	8 15	8 19	8 25	8 25	8 30	8 34	8 40	8 45
Heaton Park	7 55	8 2	8 7	.	8 17	8 21	8 27	8 27	.	8 36	8 42	8 47
Bowker Vale	7 57	8 4	8 9	...	8 19	8 23	8 29	8 29	...	8 38	8 44	8 49
Crumpsall	7 59	8 6	8 11	.	8 21	8 25	8 31	8 31	.	8 40	8 46	8 51
Woodlands Road	...	8 8	8 13	...	8 23	8 27	8 33	8 33	8 36	8 42	8 48	8 53
Manchester (Victoria) arr	8 5	8 13	8 18	8 20	8 28	8 32	8 38	8 38	8 41	8 47	8 53	8 58

	a.m.		a.m.	a.m.	a.m.	a.m.		a.m.	a.m.	SO a.m.
145 Bacup dep	.	.	.	8 30	9* 0	.	.	.	10 15	.
Bury (Bolton Street) dep	8 43	...	9 0	9 22	9 40	10 10	...	10 40	11 10	11 30
Radcliffe (Central) "	8 47	.	9 4	9 26	9 44	10 14	.	10 44	11 14	11 34
Whitefield	8 50	...	9 7	9 29	9 47	10 17	...	10 47	11 17	11 37
Besses-o'th'-Barn	8 52	.	9 9	9 31	9 49	10 19	.	10 49	11 19	11 39
Prestwich	8 53	...	9 10	9 32	9 50	10 20	...	10 50	11 20	11 40
Heaton Park	8 55	.	9 12	9 34	9 52	10 22	.	10 52	11 22	11 42
Bowker Vale	8 57	...	9 14	9 36	9 54	10 24	...	10 54	11 24	11 44
Crumpsall	8 59	.	9 16	9 38	9 56	10 26	.	10 56	11 26	11 46
Woodlands Road	9 1	...	9 18	9 40	9 58	10 28	...	10 58	11 28	11 48
Manchester (Victoria) arr	9 6	.	9 23	9 45	10 3	10 34	.	11 3	11 33	11 53

WEEKDAYS — continued.

	SO noon	noon	SO p.m.	SX p.m.		SO p.m.	p.m.	SO p.m.	SX p.m.	SO p.m.	SO p.m.	p.m.
145 Bacup dep	.	.	.	.	.	.	.	.	.	.	.	12 18
Bury (Bolton Street) dep	...	12 0	12 10	12 17	...	12 20	12 30	12 40	12 45	...	12 50	1 0
Radcliffe (Central) "	.	12 4	12 14	12 21	.	12 24	12 34	12 44	12 49	.	12 54	1 4
Whitefield	...	12 7	12 17	12 24	...	12 27	12 37	12 47	12 52	...	12 57	1 7
Besses-o'th'-Barn	.	12 9	12 19	12 26	.	12 29	12 39	12 49	12 54	.	12 59	1 9
Prestwich	12 0	12 10	12 20	12 27	...	12 30	12 40	12 50	12 55	12 55	1 0	1 10
Heaton Park	12 2	12 12	12 22	12 29	.	12 32	12 42	12 52	12 57	12 57	1 2	1 12
Bowker Vale	12 4	12 14	12 24	12 31	...	12 34	12 44	12 54	12 59	12 59	1 4	1 14
Crumpsall	12 6	12 16	12 26	12 33	.	12 36	12 46	12 56	1 1	1 1	1 6	1 16
Woodlands Road	12 8	12 18	12 28	12 35	...	12 38	12 48	12 58	1 3	1 3	1 8	1 18
Manchester (Victoria) arr	12 13	12 23	12 33	12 40	.	12 43	12 53	1 3	1 8	1 8	1 13	1 23

		SO p.m.	SX p.m.		SO p.m.	p.m.	SO p.m.	SX p.m.		SO p.m.	p.m.	p.m.
145 Bacup dep	.	.	.	.	.	.	.	1 10	.	1 10	.	.
Bury (Bolton Street) dep	...	1 14	1 15	...	1 22	1 30	1 40	1 45	...	1 50	2 0	2 20
Radcliffe (Central) "	.	1 18	1 19	.	1 26	1 34	1 44	1 49	.	1 54	2 4	2 24
Whitefield	...	1 21	1 22	...	1 29	1 37	1 47	1 52	...	1 57	2 7	2 27
Besses-o'th'-Barn	.	1 23	1 24	.	1 31	1 39	1 49	1 54	.	1 59	2 9	2 29
Prestwich	...	1 24	1 25	...	1 32	1 40	1 50	1 55	...	2 0	2 10	2 30
Heaton Park	.	1 26	1 27	.	1 34	1 42	1 52	1 57	.	2 2	2 12	2 32
Bowker Vale	...	1 28	1 29	...	1 36	1 44	1 54	1 59	...	2 4	2 14	2 34
Crumpsall	.	1 30	1 31	.	1 38	1 46	1 56	2 1	.	2 6	2 16	2 36
Woodlands Road	...	1 32	1 33	...	1 40	1 48	1 58	2 3	...	2 8	2 18	2 38
Manchester (Victoria) arr	.	1 37	1 38	.	1 45	1 53	2 3	2 8	.	2 13	2 23	2 43

	p.m.	SO p.m.	SX p.m.	SO p.m.		p.m.	SO p.m.	SX p.m.	p.m.	p.m.	SX p.m.
145 Bacup dep	2 3	2 20	.	.	.	3SO0	.	.	.	3 54	.
Bury (Bolton Street) dep	2 40	3 0	3 10	3 20	...	3 40	4 0	4 10	4 20	4 40	...
Radcliffe (Central) "	2 44	3 4	3 14	3 24	.	3 44	4 4	4 14	4 24	4 44	.
Whitefield	2 47	3 7	3 17	3 27	...	3 47	4 7	4 17	4 27	4 47	...
Besses-o'th'-Barn	2 49	3 9	3 19	3 29	.	3 49	4 9	4 19	4 29	4 49	.
Prestwich	2 50	3 10	3 20	3 30	...	3 50	4 10	4 20	4 30	4 50	4 55
Heaton Park	2 52	3 12	3 22	3 32	.	3 52	4 12	4 22	4 32	4 52	4 57
Bowker Vale	2 54	3 14	3 24	3 34	...	3 54	4 14	4 24	4 34	4 54	4 59
Crumpsall	2 56	3 16	3 26	3 36	.	3 56	4 16	4 26	4 36	4 56	5 1
Woodlands Road	2 58	3 18	3 28	3 38	...	3 58	4 18	4 28	4 38	4 58	5 3
Manchester (Victoria) arr	3 3	3 23	3 33	3 43	.	4 3	4 23	4 33	4 43	5 3	5 8

✱—Third class only. SO—Saturdays only. SX—Saturdays excepted.

A 1950 timetable for local trains operating between Victoria and Bury. When the ELR line to Bury was opened, their trains made use of Victoria until a disagreement over tolls from Salford forced the ELR to use another terminus at Salford. This situation remained until the ELR amalgamated with the LYR in 1859 and Bury trains were transferred back to Victoria.

The LYR Whitefield station, on the line between Manchester Victoria and Bolton, with an electric tram passing by. Below the station name an advertisement for season tickets to Manchester states that 'a yearly season ticket for any number of journeys TO MANCHESTER for 7½d per day 1st Class and 5d 3rd Class'. Other stations on the line were Woodland Road, Crumpsall, Heaton Park, Prestwich, Besses O'Th' Barn, Radcliffe, Ainsworth Road, Bradley Fold, Darcey Lever, and Bolton (Trinity Street).

The station at Bolton in the 1980s. Bolton was famous as a manufacturer of textiles for over 400 years, initially woollen fabrics and later cotton goods. The town was also involved in the manufacture of textile machinery, Isaac Dobson starting production of such machinery in 1790. Railway locomotives were built in the town when Hick Hargreaves founded a works there in 1833. The company built railway engines in Bolton until 1855 when they turned over to cotton mill machinery. Another company, Rothwells, continued loco building in the town for several years afterwards, manufacturing some broad gauge 'Singles' for the Great Western Railway. The Manchester, Bolton & Bury Canal Navigation and Railway Company began operations to Bolton in 1845 with a service of ten trains each way per day. Fares were 2s 6d first class and 1s 6d second class. Its Bolton terminus was at the site of what was to become Trinity Street, and trains operated on the right hand side until the East Lancashire Railway line was opened, forcing the MB & B to move operations to the left. Bolton was not a terminus for long and within a decade it became a major junction. A line from Manchester had been extended to Preston and Blackburn and lines from Liverpool and Wigan also entered the station. By 1850 Bolton station was one of the busiest junction on the LYR system, with trains converging from Manchester, Rochdale, Yorkshire, Liverpool, Wigan, Preston and Blackburn.

The main platform at Bolton station in the 1980s. The station was improved in the late 1980s at a cost of some £3 million.

Moses Gate station, Bolton, in the 1920s. The station was situated on the Bolton (Trinity Street) to Manchester (Victoria) line, running via Clifton Junction and Salford.

Oldham Werneth station, on the LYR line from Manchester Victoria. The first station at Werneth was opened in 1842 and had a single all-over roof, but this was dismantled in the 1880s when the station was rebuilt.

Oldham Werneth station in 1956. The station was at the top of a 1 in 27 incline to Central station and a branch to Hollinwood also had an incline of 1 in 50. This view shows the west end of the station with the footbridge, built in 1884, which linked with a bridge leading to its Featherstall Road entrance.

The LYR line at Shaw, with the Jubilee Colliery next to the railway. The road was built with the railway in 1863 and has been the source of traffic congestion for many years.

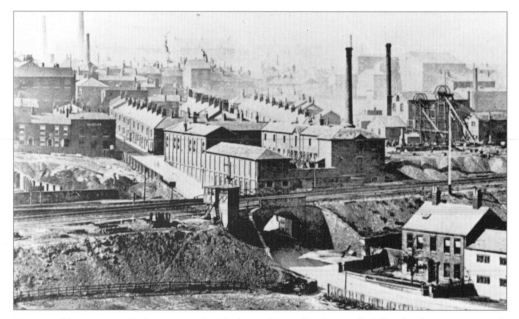

Dominated by cotton mill chimneys and coal mines, this is the throat of Oldham's Clegg Street Goods Yard. The Waterloo Street railway bridge carries the LYR and the Oldham, Ashton & Guide Bridge Railway tracks into the town. The existence of the OA & GBR brought the Great Central Railway into Oldham and, after 'Grouping', the town was served by both the LMS and LNER.

The massive goods yard at Clegg Street, which belonged to the OA & GBR, *c*. 1890. On the extreme left is the warehouse of the MS & L with its newly-built office block overlooking the yard. Just out of view to the right is the LNWR warehouse. There are many 'private owner' wagons in this view, most full of coal and lime for building use. In the background are cotton mills and rows of terraced houses which housed mill workers.

The terminus station at Royton, Oldham, in the 1920s. This single platform terminus was opened on 21 March 1864. Although at first served by a single line, Royton was provided with extensive goods facilities, including its own cotton warehouse and goods shed. During the late 1950s and early 1960s, redundant railway coaches, including sleeping cars and suburban rolling stock, were brought to Royton goods yard for scrapping. The coach bodies were scrapped, but the underframes were retained for conversion into car carrying vehicles for use on 'Motorail' trains. Nearby Lees shed provided an Austerity 2–8–0 loco to Royton for handling the huge quantity of old coaches.

Table 148

MANCHESTER, OLDHAM, ROYTON AND ROCHDALE

WEEKDAYS

Miles		
0	Manchester (Victoria) .... dep	
1¼	Miles Platting	
2½	Dean Lane, Newton Heath	
3¾	Failsworth	
4½	Hollinwood	
0	Middleton Junction .... dep	
6¼ 1	Oldham (Werneth)	
7¼	" (Central)	
7½	" (Mumps) .... dep	
8¼ 0	Royton Junction	
1	Royton	
10¼	Shaw and Crompton .... dep	
12	New Hey	
12¾	Milnrow	
14½	Rochdale .... arr	

(WEEKDAYS—continued)

(SUNDAYS)

For other Train Services between Manchester (Victoria), Miles Platting, and Newton Heath, see Tables 117, 120 and 145.

A Arrives five minutes earlier.   B—Passengers change at Middleton Junction.   C—Newton Heath Station.   K—Arrives Shaw 7-56 a.m.   SO—Saturdays only.   SX—Saturdays excepted.

Table 148—continued

ROCHDALE, ROYTON, OLDHAM AND MANCHESTER

WEEKDAYS

Miles		
0	Rochdale .... dep	
2	Milnrow	
2¾	New Hey	
4½	Shaw and Crompton	
0	Royton .... dep	
6¼ 1	Royton Junction	
7¼	Oldham (Mumps) .... dep	
7½	" (Central)	
8¼	" (Werneth)	
1¼	Middleton Junction .... arr	
10	Hollinwood .... dep	
11	Failsworth	
12	Dean Lane, Newton Heath	
13½	Miles Platting	
14½	Manchester (Victoria) ...... arr	

(WEEKDAYS — continued)

(SUNDAYS)

For other Train Services between Manchester (Victoria), Miles Platting, and Newton Heath, see Tables 117, 120 and 145.

A Arrives five minutes earlier.   B—Passengers change at Middleton Junction.   C—Newton Heath Station.   K—Arrives Shaw 7-56 a.m.   SO—Saturdays only.   SX—Saturdays excepted.

A January 1950 timetable for ex-LYR services between Manchester Victoria and Rochdale, via Oldham.

The exterior of the LYR station at Bootle, on the line from Liverpool Exchange to Southport, opened on 20 November 1848. This line met the East Lancashire Railway line from Southport to Preston, which was opened on 2 April 1849.

The interior of Bootle station after the line was electrified. This work, between Liverpool Exchange and Southport, was completed in 1904 with the first electric services commencing in March of that year. Once fully operational, there were some sixty-three trains running per day, compared with thirty-six in steam days.

Crosby station, also on the LYR electrified line to Southport.

Hightown station near Formby, on the route to Southport, complete with enamel advertisements on the fence, substantial LYR station building and electrified track with an electric train leaving the station.

Formby station shortly after electrification with, unusually, a steam train approaching the station. Note the station boards informing passengers where to stand for first or third class smoking or non-smoking coaches.

A modern view of ex-LYR Ainsdale station, still on the Southport line.

The Lakeside Miniature Railway at Southport, busy with passengers during the summer months. The seaside town was developed rapidly with the arrival of the railways. The West Lancashire Railway, absorbed by the LYR in July 1897, arrived here in 1883 to a terminus at Southport Central. The LYR had its own line, via Formby, to Southport Chapel Street, and the Cheshire Lines Committee also had a round about route to Southport Lord Street which opened in September 1884.

Llewelyn's Miniature Railway at Southport at the turn of the century. Nowadays, only the Merseyrail system operates to Southport.

Table 149

LIVERPOOL, AINTREE, ORMSKIRK AND PRESTON

WEEKDAYS

Miles.		a.m.	a.m.		a.m.	a.m.		a.m.	a.m.	a.m.		a.m.	a.m.	
0	Liverpool (Exchange) ... dep													
1¼	Sandhills													
2½	Kirkdale													
	Walton Junction													
3½	Preston Road .... arr													
	Orrell Park .... dep													
	Aintree													
	Old Roan													
	Maghull													
	Town Green and Aughton....													
	Aughton Park													
	Ormskirk													
	Burscough Junction .... arr													
	124 Southport arr													
	124, 144 (Chapel St.) dep													
	Burscough Junction ..... dep													
7½	Rufford													
10½	Croston													
13	Midge Hall													
15½	Lostock Hall													
16½	Preston Junction													
20½	Preston .... arr													

WEEKDAYS — continued

	a.m.	a.m.	a.m.	a.m.	a.m.	a.m.	p.m.	p.m.	p.m.	p.m.
Liverpool (Exchange) ... dep										
Sandhills										
Kirkdale										
Walton Junction										
Preston Road .... arr										
Orrell Park .... dep										
Aintree										
Old Roan										
Maghull										
Town Green and Aughton....										
Aughton Park										
Ormskirk										
Burscough Junction .... arr										
124 Southport arr										
124, 144 (Chapel St.) dep										
Burscough Junction ..... dep										
Rufford										
Croston										
Midge Hall										
Lostock Hall										
Preston Junction ...... arr										
Preston .... arr										

For Notes see Page 386.

Table 149
continued.

LIVERPOOL, AINTREE, ORMSKIRK AND PRESTON

WEEKDAYS — continued.

	p.m.	p.m.	p.m.	p.m.	p.m.	p.m.	p.m.	p.m.	p.m.	p.m.
Liverpool (Exchange) ... dep										
Sandhills										
Kirkdale										
Walton Junction										
Preston Road .... arr										
Orrell Park .... dep										
Aintree										
Old Roan										
Maghull										
Town Green and Aughton....										
Aughton Park										
Ormskirk										
Burscough Junction .... arr										
124 Southport arr										
124, 144 (Chapel St.) dep										
Burscough Junction ..... dep										
Rufford										
Croston										
Midge Hall										
Lostock Hall										
Preston Junction ...... arr										
Preston .... arr										

WEEKDAYS — continued.

	p.m.	p.m.	p.m.	p.m.	p.m.	p.m.	p.m.	p.m.	p.m.
Liverpool (Exchange) ... dep									
Sandhills									
Kirkdale									
Walton Junction									
Preston Road .... arr									
Orrell Park .... dep									
Aintree									
Old Roan									
Maghull									
Town Green and Aughton....									
Aughton Park									
Ormskirk									
Burscough Junction .... arr									
124 Southport arr									
124, 144 (Chapel St.) dep									
Burscough Junction ..... dep									
Croston									
Midge Hall									
Lostock Hall									
Preston Junction ...... arr									
Preston .... arr									

For Notes see Page 386.

A 1950s timetable for trains from Liverpool Exchange to Preston, via Ormskirk.

Orrell Park station, on the ex-ELR line from Liverpool Exchange to Preston, complete with LYR electric train, the LYR having absorbed the ELR in 1859.

Orrell Park station as it appeared in LYR days. The ELR met the LYR at Walton for access to Liverpool where, despite later bitter rivalry, the two companies had a joint station opened in 1848. They could not agree on a name – it was Great Howard Street to the ELR and Borough Gaol to the LYR. Very soon afterwards a new Liverpool Joint station was built, ½ mile nearer to the city centre, known as Exchange to the LYR and Tithebarn Street to the ELR. The station had two of everything, including two iron roofs. After amalgamation a new Exchange station, designed by Sir John Hawkshaw in 'Italianate Style', was opened in 1884–8.

The station at Orrell Park in LMS days, opened by the ELR in 1849. The station remains open to suburban traffic operating between Liverpool Central and Ormskirk, the LYR station at Liverpool Exchange having closed on 30 April 1977, when all trains began to run through to Central station on the Merseyrail system.

Railway bridges crossing the River Ribble at Preston, the town being a major junction between the LYR and the LNWR.

Entrance to Preston station at Fishergate in early BR days. Event the motor cars in this view are as much a part of history as the steam locomotives operating out of Preston all those years ago. The first railway to come to Preston was the Preston & Wigan Railway, authorized in 1831, which merged with the Wigan Branch Railway to form the North Union Railway in 1834. The Bolton & Preston Railway became part of the NUR in 1844. By 1846 the NUR had been vested in the Grand Junction Railway and the Manchester & Leeds Railway. Thus, the company was to become the joint property of the LNWR and LYR. Another company, the ELR, also came to Preston in 1846, becoming another constituent of the LYR from 1859. Despite much early politicking, the two companies settled down to an amicable working relationship at Preston, and the town became an important junction. Its most important line is the ex-LNWR West Coast Main Line, now fully electrified from Euston to Glasgow.

The interior of Preston station, which opened in 1880, replacing the more ramshackle structure that had sufficed since the railway first came to the town. Efforts had been made to improve what was a rather inconvenient and dangerous station, passengers having to cross from one platform to another over the railway lines. In 1856 a Bill was presented to parliament for station improvements, but the companies could not agree and it was rejected. On 18 August 1866 part of the roof on the ELR section of the station fell in, injuring two porters and a woman passenger. This brought more complaints about the state of the station but it was not until the 1870s that a new building was begun. This new station cost £250,000 and came into use in July 1880.

SOUTHPORT TO PRESTON

Mls.		WEEKDAYS																			
											SX			SO							
		a.m.	a.m.	a.m.	a.m. (TC to Todmorden, arrive 9-46 a.m. (Table 153))	a.m.	a.m.	a.m.	a.m.	a.m.	a.m. (TC to Blackpool (Cen.) arrive 11-35 a.m. (Table 140))	a.m.		p.m.	p.m.	p.m.		p.m.	p.m.	p.m.	p.m.
0	Southport – Chapel Street ....dep	5 45	6 20	7 0	8 0	8 5	8 29	8 45	9 35	10 0	10 30	11 15	.	12 18	12 42	1 48	.	2 55	3 30	4 12	5
¾	Southport – St. Luke's	5 48	6 23	7 3	8 3	8 8	8 32	8 48	9 38	10 3	10 33	11 18	...	12 21	12 45	1 51	...	2 58	3 33	4 15	5 [illegible]
1¾	Hesketh Park	5 51	6 26	7 6	8 6	8 11	8 35	8 51	9 41	.		11 21	.	12 24	12 48	1 54	.	3 1	3 36	4 18	5 [illegible]
2½	Churchtown	5 53	6 28	7 8	8 8	8 13	8 37	8 53	9 43	10 6		11 23	...	12 26	12 50	1 56	...	3 4	3 38	4 20	5 [illegible]
3	Crossens	5 55	6 30	7 10	.	8 15	.	8 55	9 45	.		11 25	.	12 28	12 52	1 58	.	3 6	3 40	4 22	5 [illegible]
4½	Banks	5 59	6 34	7 14	...	8 19	...	8 59	9 49	10 10		11 29	...	12 32	12 56	2 2	...	3 10	3 44	4 26	5 [illegible]
6½	Hundred End	6 3	6 38	.	.	8 23	.	9 3	9 53	.		11 33	.	12 36	1 0	2 6	.	3 14	3 48	4 30	5 [illegible]
8¼	Hesketh Bank	6 7	6 42	7 20	8 16	8 27	...	9 7	9 57	10 16		11 37	...	12 40	1 4	2 10	...	3 18	3 52	4 34	5 [illegible]
9¾	Hoole	6 11	6 46	7 24	.	8 31	.	9 11	10 1	.		11 41	.	12 44	1 8	2 14	.	3 22	3 56	4 38	5 [illegible]
11	Longton Bridge	6 14	6 49	7 27	8 21	8 34	...	9 14	10 4	10 21		11 44	...	12 47	1 11	2 17	...	3 25	3 59	4 41	5 [illegible]
12¾	New Longton and Hutton............	6 18	6 53	7 31	.	8 38	.	9 18	10 8	10 25		11 48	.	12 51	1 15	2 21	.	3 29	4 3	4 45	5 [illegible]
14	Penwortham (Cop Lane).............	6 21	6 56	7 34	...	8 41	...	9 21	10 11	...		11 51	...	12 54	1 18	2 24	...	3 32	4 6	4 48	5 [illegible]
16	Preston ....arr	6 27	7 2	7 40	.	8 47	8 57	9 27	10 17	10 32	11 0	11 57	.	1 0	1 24	2 30	.	3 38	4 12	4 54	5 [illegible]

A timetable for trains operating between Southport and Preston, over the old ELR route.

One of Preston station's platform signals, with pigeons in baskets on a porter's trolley. These trolleys were a common feature at main railway stations in steam days. Where, I wonder, were the pigeons bound?

Jointly owned by the LNWR and LYR, the Park Hotel at Preston is pictured in 1896. It was designed by Arnold Mitchell and opened in 1882.

Ex-LMS 'Black Five' no. 44737 at Preston station at the head of a train from Liverpool in 1965. Preston was one of the last strongholds of steam traction, which finally disappeared from the town in 1968.

Prototype English-Electric 3300 h.p. Co-Co diesel-electric loco 'Deltic' leaving Preston in 1955. The loco was an unusual sight at Preston, as the engine was normally used on expresses operating over the WCML between Euston and Liverpool (Lime Street).

Another long disappeared diesel loco at Preston is Metropolitan Vickers Co-Bo no. D5703 in the early 1960s. These engines were not very successful and had gone by the early 1970s.

Mill Hill station, on the LYR line from Preston to Blackburn, built jointly with the Lancashire Union Railway. The line was opened in 1868 and by an Act of 1883 the LUR was vested in the LNWR, so the line became jointly owned by the LYR and LNWR.

The station square at Blackburn in 1925. Buses, trams and taxis give an indication of how busy the station was in those days.

The platforms at Blackburn station. The town was famous for its cotton mills and by 1867 there were 107 spinning and weaving mills in the Blackburn area. The Leeds & Liverpool Canal reached Blackburn in 1816 and the first railway, the Blackburn & Preston Railway, opened in 1846. The ELR arrived in 1848 when it opened its line to Accrington. Another line, the Blackburn, Darwen & Bolton Railway, opened in 1847 and was designed to provide a shorter link to Manchester. The most important town on its route was Darwen.

Table 142

WIGAN AND BLACKBURN

A 1950s timetable for trains operating between Wigan and Blackburn.

Ex-LMS 7F 0–8–0 freight engine no. 49515 (the class being familiarly known as 'Austin Sevens'), outside the LYR shed at Wigan. This shed, coded 27B in BR days, supplied locos for local passenger and freight work as its allocation for 30 January 1954 shows:

LMS 2P 4–4–0: 40587, 40680
LMS Fairburn 2–6–4T: 42180, 42297, 42299
LMS Stanier 2–6–4T: 42537, 42554, 42557, 42569, 42592, 42614, 42631, 42632, 42640, 42641, 42642, 42644
MR 4F 0–6–0: 43952
LMS 4F 0–6–0: 44105, 44220, 44221, 44225, 44240, 44464, 44544
LMS Fowler 0–8–0: 49592, 49598
LYR Barton-Wright 2F 0–6–0: 51474
LYR Aspinall 3F 0–6–0: 52095, 52197, 52275, 52289, 52387, 52450
WD 'Austerity' 2–8–0: 90121, 90570, 90671
Total: 37

The LNWR also served Wigan and had a large locoshed at Springs Branch, coded 10A until becoming a sub-shed of Liverpool Edge Hill in 1958 when it was recoded 8F. Like the LYR shed, Springs Branch also provided freight and local passenger locos, the allocation for the same day provides evidence of this:

LMS Fairburn 2–6–4T: 42266
LMS Stanier 2–6–4T: 42453, 42454, 42456, 42462, 42465, 42539, 42572, 42610, 42663, 42666
LMS Ivatt Class 2 2–6–0: 46428, 46432, 46434
LMS 'Black Five' 4–6–0: 45004, 45026, 45055, 45135, 45289, 45313, 45314, 45408, 45425, 45449, 45454
LNWR 7F 0–8–0: 48895, 49007, 49018, 49023, 49025, 49129, 49154, 49160, 49228, 49268, 49306, 49311, 49322, 49341, 49352, 49378, 49381, 49385, 49393, 49401, 49402, 49408, 49436
LYR Barton-Wright 2F 0–6–0: 52021, 52051
LYR Aspinall 3F 0–6–0: 52118, 52143, 52322, 52341, 52449, 52551
GC J10 0–6–0: 65148, 65159, 65162, 65173, 65175, 65176, 65199, 65203
Total: 64

An 1890s view of Chorley station, situated on the Bolton and Preston Railway. An Act to build the B & PR was obtained on 15 June 1837 and the first section, from an end-on junction with the Bolton–Manchester line, was opened to a temporary terminus, 9½ miles away at Rawlinson Bridge. By 22 December the new line reached Chorley and Rawlinson Bridge ceased to exist. The new line was worked by the Manchester, Bolton & Bury Railway from the outset, using 2–2–0 and 0–4–0 locos built by Edward Bury and Fairbairn. The line was opened to Preston on 22 June 1843 and became a part of the LYR in 1889. The bridge crossing the line in this view was replaced by a subway in the twentieth century. Chorley station is still very much in existence, handling local passenger trains that still operate between Bolton and Preston.

The ELR station of Church and Oswaldtwistle in LYR days. The busy scene shows two local trains in the station and an LYR loco of the day can be seen at the head of one of them. The station was on the section between Blackburn and Accrington and was named 'Church' when opened on 19 June 1848. Its full name was adopted from July 1895. The station remains open as Oswaldtwistle, and is served by DMU services between Preston and Colne.

The junction station at Accrington opened in 1848. The station served trains from Blackburn to Nelson and Colne and to Bury, part of which has now been preserved as the East Lancs Railway.

From Accrington, the ELR built a line northwards to Colne, opening to a temporary terminus at Burnley (Westgate) on 18 September 1848. The extension to Colne was opened on 1 February 1849 and a new Burnley station was opened nearer to the centre of the town. The temporary station was closed, only to re-open as Burnley Barracks in September 1851. The new station, pictured here, was named Burnley Bank Top from 1870 until 1944, when it became Burnley Central.

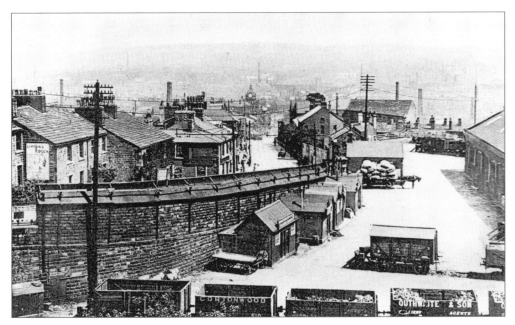

The town of Burnley from Spring Hill, with the goods siding full of private owner wagons on the right.

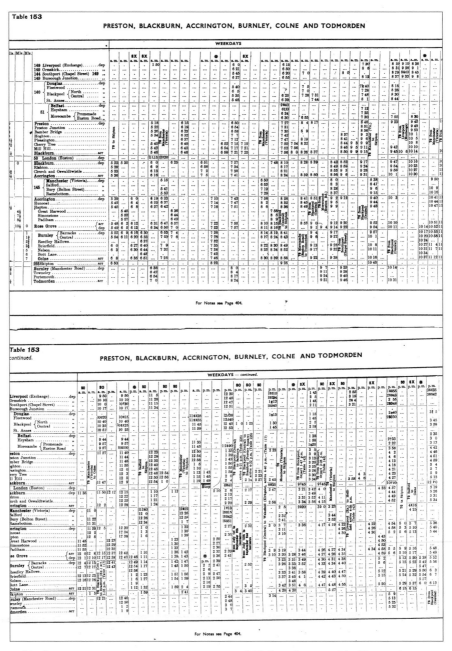

A timetable for trains operating between Preston and Todmorden, via Blackburn, Accrington and Burnley.

The old ELR line from Bury to Accrington via Rawtenstall was closed to passengers in 1972, but remained open to coal traffic until December 1980. In the meantime, the East Lancashire Railway Preservation Society was thinking of using the section from Stubbins Junction to Haslington to operate steam trains. However, they were confined to a depot in Bury for many years until funding by Greater Manchester Council allowed re-opening of the section between Bury and Rawtenstall in the early 1990s.

Ex-LNER A3 Pacific no. 4472 'Flying Scotsman' is seen at Rossendale with an excursion train.

'Flying Scotsman' running tender first over the Bury–Rawtenstall section of the ELR. In the days when the society was confined to Bury, they owned several industrial and main line diesel locos, as the following list shows:

D832 'Onslaught' BR Class 42 Bo-Bo, built 1961
D1041 'Western Lady' BR Class 52 Co-Co, built 1962
32 'Gothenburg' Hudswell-Clarke 0–6–0T, built 1903
70 Hudswell-Clarke 0–6–0T, built 1921
945 Barclay 0–4–0ST, built 1904
1 Barclay 0–4–0ST, built 1927
MEA No 1 RSH 0–6–0T, built 1951

The society also had one BR Mk 1 coach, and one ex-LYR coach and a number of small freight wagons, along with two four-wheel diesel mechanical locos.

The entrance to Blackpool Central station, one of three that served the holiday mecca of the north-west, as it appeared at the turn of the century. Central station was served by a line from Preston and was jointly owned by the LYR and LNWR who had taken control of the Preston & Wyre Railway in 1871.

Blackpool Central entrance in early BR days. In the summer months the station was intensively used by excursion trains, many hundreds of which were run in conjunction with the 'Wakes Weeks', when whole towns' cotton mills closed for a week. By the 1950s excursion trains were run from further afield, putting even more pressure on the railways in the town. The other two stations, Blackpool North (which still exists) and Blackpool South, were also busy, but Central station was busiest as it was sited close to the sea front.

The station throat at Blackpool Central, with Blackpool Tower behind the station, a sight that must have brought excitement to many a child after a long rail trip to the seaside.

Table 141

FLEETWOOD TO BLACKPOOL

WEEKDAYS

Miles		
0	Fleetwood .... dep	
¼	Wyre Dock	
3¼	Burn Naze	
4¼	Thornton (for Cleveleys)	
	Poulton .... arr	
6	Poulton Curve .... dep	
7½	Layton (Lancs.)	
9	Blackpool (North) .... arr	

WEEKDAYS — continued.

Fleetwood .... dep	
Wyre Dock	
Burn Naze	
Thornton (for Cleveleys)	
Poulton .... arr	
Poulton Curve .... dep	
Layton (Lancs.)	
Blackpool (North) .... arr	

W'DAYS — contd.   SUNDAYS

Fleetwood .... dep	
Wyre Dock	
Burn Naze	
Thornton (for Cleveleys)	
Poulton .... dep	
Poulton Curve	
Layton (Lancs.)	
Blackpool (North) .... arr	

B—Arrives five minutes earlier.   MX—Mondays excepted.   SO—Saturdays only.   SX—Saturdays excepted.

Table 141 — continued

BLACKPOOL TO FLEETWOOD

WEEKDAYS

Miles		
0	Blackpool (North) .... dep	
1½	Layton (Lancs.)	
3	Poulton Curve	
	Poulton .... arr	
	Poulton .... dep	
4½	Thornton (for Cleveleys)	
5½	Burn Naze	
8½	Wyre Dock	
9	Fleetwood .... arr	

WEEKDAYS — continued.

Blackpool (North) .... dep	
Layton (Lancs.)	
Poulton Curve	
Poulton .... arr	
Poulton .... dep	
Thornton (for Cleveleys)	
Burn Naze	
Wyre Dock	
Fleetwood .... arr	

W'DAYS — contd.   SUNDAYS

Blackpool (North) .... dep	
Layton (Lancs.)	
Poulton Curve	
Poulton .... arr	
Poulton	
Thornton (for Cleveleys)	
Burn Naze	
Wyre Dock	
Fleetwood	

B—Arrives five minutes earlier.   MX—Mondays excepted.   SO—Saturdays only.   SX—Saturdays excepted.

A 1950s timetable for local trains operating from Blackpool North to Fleetwood.

A general view of Blackpool Central station with centre platform faces full of coaches and train awaiting departure.

A local train operating between Central and Lytham St Anne's (known as the home of the Football Association), operated by an LMS diesel-electric set.

The LYR works at Horwich built all the locomotives for the needs of the company and beyond, until it was closed in 1983. The first engines, built at the works between 1889 and 1910, were 2–4–2 tank locos. This example, no. 816, had 18 x 26 in cylinders, 5 ft 8 in diameter driving wheels and was worked at 180 lb steam pressure. This loco was built in 1905.

LYR combined engine and coach, called a 'Railmotor' no. 8, one of a batch built between 1906 and 1911 for use on local trains. The loco had 12 x 16 in cylinders and 3 ft 7⅝ in driving wheels, and worked at a pressure of 180 lb per square inch. The last of these little sets was withdrawn in 1948.

LYR superheated 4–4–0 bogie passenger engine no. 1098, built in 1909. The class had 20 x 26 in cylinders, 7 ft 3 in driving wheels and a steam pressure of 180 lb. None of these engines survived to come into BR ownership.

LYR 4–4–2 bogie passenger loco no. 1406, built in 1902. These locos had 19 x 26 in cylinders, 7 ft 3 in driving wheels, and a boiler pressure of 180 lb.

LYR 'Dreadnought' class 4–6–0 no. 1510, built in 1908. This loco and her sisters, a total of seventy-five in all, were designed by Hughes. Built between 1908 and 1925, they were used on 'top-link' expresses over the LYR routes and were a common sight at Blackpool Central over the years. These locos had 16 x 26 in cylinders, 6 ft 3 in driving wheels, and 180 lb boiler pressure. All of these handsome engines had been withdrawn by 1951.

LYR compound 0–8–0 goods engine no. 1471, built at Horwich in 1907. These engines were used for heavy freight work, hauling coal and cotton throughout Lancashire until replaced by LMS Stanier 8F 2–8–0s and ex-LNWR 0–8–0s. These engines had 15½ in and 22 x 26 in cylinders, 4 ft 6 in driving wheels and a boiler pressure of 180 lb.

A little LYR 0–4–0 saddle tank loco, known as a 'pug'. These engines were built between 1891 and 1910 for use as dock shunters, and many of these little engines could be found in the dock areas of Liverpool and Birkenhead. By 1948 twenty-three were still in use and continued to be fully utilized until withdrawal began in 1956. Despite this, some remained in use until 1964 when the final ones disappeared. Two of these engines, BR nos 51218 and 51243, have found their way into preservation as a reminder of the days when the Mersey had massive dock complexes and little tank locos shuffled up and down dock lines shunting many thousands of wagons over the years.

THE GREAT CENTRAL RAILWAY AND CHESHIRE LINES COMMITTEE

The LNER gained access to Manchester by the absorption of the Great Central Railway, following the 'Grouping' of 1923. The GCR came into existence in 1907, and the Manchester, Sheffield, and Lincolnshire Railway was one of the constituents of the new company, hence the Manchester connection. Its main line ran from Manchester to Sheffield and London (Marylebone).

The company's Lancashire terminus was at Manchester Central, a station shared with the Cheshire Lines Committee. The CLC was a partnership between the Great Central, Great Northern, and Midland Railways. The company had a direct route from Manchester Central to Liverpool Central, providing a competitive route to the L & M, and a line from Chester (Foregate Street) to Manchester Central, through sparsely populated areas of Cheshire. Access from Timperley (Cheshire) to Manchester Central was over metals of the Manchester South Junction and Altrincham Railway, which was jointly owned by the Great Central and LNWR.

Locomotives from the LNER provided variety and contrast to the usual mix of LMS types that predominated traffic in Lancashire.

Manchester, Sheffield & Lincolnshire Railway 2–2–2 loco no. 501 at Manchester Central station at the turn of the century. The engine, which became Great Central Railway stock in 1907, was built at Gorton works in 1883. Manchester Central station came into existence following the forced quitting of the Midland Railway from the LNWR London Road station in the 1860s. Central station actually opened on 9 July 1877 and was used by the Cheshire Lines Committee which immediately introduced an express service to Liverpool Central (journey time of forty-five minutes) running every hour. The CLC was formed by the merger of GNR, MS & L and MR in 1865. Central station was initially only a temporary affair; the permanent station actually opened on 1 July 1880. This new station comprised an arched roof with a 210 ft span and walls that were no more than screens on either side. Offices and waiting rooms were built of timber because plans had been made to build an hotel adjoining the station, but it came to nothing. The timber buildings, however, remained. Withdrawal of ex-GCR services in 1958, and diversion of MR trains in 1967, left Central with only CLC Liverpool trains. These trains were transferred to Oxford Road and Central station was closed on 5 May 1969.

Table 80   **MANCHESTER (Central), FALLOWFIELD, and GUIDE BRIDGE**

Miles		Week Days				Suns	
		am	a.m	non pm S E	pm pm E	p.m	a.m pm
—	Manchester(Central) .. dep	736	1040	.. 12 0 410	.. 527 543	.. 1055 ..	.. 1025 530
3¼	Chorlton-cum-Hardy.......	743	..	12 8 417	 550	.. ..	.. .. ..
4½	Wilbraham Road..........	746	..	1213 420	 553	.. ..	.. .. ..
5½	Fallowfield A	750	..	1218 424	 557	.. ..	.. .. ..
7	Levenshulme	755	..	1223 428	.. 6 1 ..	.. ..	.. .. ..
8½	Hyde Road...............	8 2	..	1230 435	.. 6 8 ..	.. ..	.. .. ..
9½	Fairfield, for Droylsden....	8 6	..	1233 438	.. 611 ..	.. ..	.. .. ..
11¼	Guide Bridge.......... arr	810	11 3	.. 1237 442	.. 553 615	.. 1058 ..	.. 1048 553

	Week Days					Suns	
	am am a.m	p.m	pm pm S E	pm		p.m pm
Guide Bridge........... dep	732 843 9 50	.. 1236	.. 321 6 4	.. 739	.. 1246 741
Fairfield for Droylsden.....	736 847 ..	.. ..	.. .. 6 8	.. ..	.. .. ..
Hyde Road	739 850 ..	.. ..	 611	.. ..	.. .. ..
Levenshulme	743 854 ..	.. ..	 615	.. ..	.. .. ..
Fallowfield A	748 858 ..	.. ..	 619	.. ..	.. .. ..
Wilbraham Road	752 9 2 ..	.. ..	 623	.. ..	.. .. ..
Chorlton-cum-Hardy.......	756 9 6 ..	.. ..	 626	.. ..	.. .. ..
Manchester (Central).. arr	8 3 914 1014	.. 1256	.. 342 633	.. 8 6	.. 1 6 8 1

A For Withington and Didsbury   E Except Saturdays   S Saturdays only

For OTHER TRAINS between Manchester and Guide Bridge, see Table 77.

A timetable for services between Manchester Central and Guide Bridge in the mid-1950s.

On 17 May 1861 the MS & L and GNR obtained an Act to build a 4 mile line to link Garston with Liverpool despite strong opposition from the LNWR. Ironically, given his past, Captain Mark Huish supported the Bill against the company from whom he had recently resigned. When in LNWR employment he had vigorously opposed any company that had different interests to those at Euston, often resorting to illegal methods in his efforts to win. The following year, the MS & L and GNR were empowered to make a terminus at Brunswick Dock which opened without ceremony on 1 June 1864, omnibuses taking passengers from Brunswick Dock to James Street. A more convenient station was required, however, and on 29 July 1864, the companies were authorized a 1½ mile extension, through tunnels, to Ranelagh Street. This extension took the name of the Liverpool Central Station Railway, but it was not until 1 March 1874 that Liverpool Central station actually opened. This station, the entrance of which is pictured here, had a single-span arched roof, but this was not as large as that at Manchester Central station, opened six years later. Central station handled Manchester–Liverpool Trains of the CLC and, from 1 September 1884, also dealt with trains operating over the 31 mile line from Liverpool to Southport. This line could not really compete with the 18½ mile line of the LYR, but passenger trains were not withdrawn until 7 January 1951. From 5 September 1966 passenger trains on the CLC were diverted from Liverpool Central to Lime Street, using a short connecting curve at Allerton to reach the LNWR line. Final closure of Central station was scheduled for June 1968, but difficulties in providing an alternative bus service for the Gateacre–Central service meant that this local service was not withdrawn until 17 April 1972, Central station closing at that time.

Another picture of the entrance to Liverpool Central station. The station also had a low-level station for the Mersey Railway underground system, plans for which had been begun in 1866 when the Mersey Pneumatic Railway Company proposed a line under the River Mersey from Birkenhead to Liverpool. The company had been incorporated in 28 June, but was unable to raise sufficient capital. By an Act of 1868, pneumatic traction was abandoned in favour of steam but no progress was made on the railway until a small trial tunnel was begun in 1879, and finished in 1881. The Mersey Railway itself was completed in 1885 and a ceremonial opening, performed by the Prince of Wales, took place on 20 January 1886. Public services began on 1 February, the line running from James Street Liverpool to Green Lane Tranmere, on the Wirral. The line was extended to Rock Ferry and opened on 15 June 1891, and a branch to Birkenhead Park was opened on 2 January 1888. The low-level station at Liverpool Central was authorized in 1882 and opened on 11 January 1892. By this time, the 0–6–4 and 2–6–2 tank locos were having difficulty climbing the severe gradients of 1 in 30 and 1 in 27. Essential installation of huge steam-driven ventilation fans to draw off engine fumes also siphoned off profits, yet the tunnels remained foul. Consequently, custom fell away and the line went into liquidation in 1887, as passengers preferred to use the Mersey ferries rather than the railway. In 1900 the company raised capital to electrify the line and electric train services began operations from 3 May 1903. This was the first railway in Britain to convert to electric traction, the equipment being supplied by the Westinghouse company. Automatic signalling was introduced in 1921 and, in 1923 automatic points were installed at the buffer steps on Central low-level station, which enabled the signalbox to be closed. Nowadays, a circular service linking all electric trains runs through Central station.

Chorlton cum Hardy station, on the CLC line from Manchester Central. Just beyond the station the line makes an end-on junction with the Midland Railway's line to Derby. Midland Railway trains used this route to gain access to Manchester Central. From 6 March 1967 local services on the MR route to Central were withdrawn, and Derby trains called at Chinley and Matlock only. From 1 January 1968 what remained of these services was diverted via Marple (Cheshire) and Belle Vue to Manchester Piccadilly, the former Manchester London Road, all of which left Manchester Central with only CLC services to Liverpool until closure in 1969.

Woodley station, on the GC/MR joint line from Manchester Central to Hayfield, via Marple. The station was also a junction for the CLC line from Glazebrook to Godley Junction on the main GC line to Sheffield.

A Great Central Railway express from London (Marylebone) to Manchester Central.

Table 149a GLAZEBROOK; WIGAN and ST. HELENS

Miles		Week Days																								Sundays					
		a.m	a.m	a.m	a.m L	a.m	a.m S	p.m S	p.m	p.m	p.m	p.m E	p.m	p.m	p.m E	p.m S		p.m E	p.m E	p.m	p.m	p.m	p.m	p.m S		a.m	a.m	p.m	p.m	p.m	p.m
—	Manchester (Central) dep	5Y30	6H50	7 38	8 0	9H33	11Y10	..	1233	..	1Y35	..	3 33	..	4K5	4Y45	..	4Y57	..	3 5	7 12	8 30	9Y40	10Y45	..	5Y25	7Y25	1Y15	5 5	8 42	9 57
3	Trafford Park A .... "	5Y36	6H57	7 44	8 6	9H39	11 41	..	1239	..	1Y41	..	3 39	..	4KA11	4Y51	..	5Y 5	5 12	6 11	7 18	8 36	9Y46	10Y51	..	5Y31	7Y31	1 Y1	5 11	8 48	10 3
8¼	Irlam and Cadishead "	6 13	7H16	8 0	8 25	9H55	11 57	..	1255	..	2 14	..	3 56	..	4H52	5 15	..	5 25	5 32	6 28	7 35	8 53	1016	11 54	..	6 13	7 55	2 15	5 27	9 4	1020
9¾	Glazebrook .... "	6 17	7 24	8 4	8 29	1030	12 2	..	1 0	..	2 18	..	4 0	..	5 19	5 19	..	5 29	5 38	6 33	7 39	8 57	1020	11 58	..	6 16	7 58	2 19	5 31	9 8	1024
12	Newchurch Halt	6 23	7 30	8 12	8 35	1036	..	..	1 7	..	2 24	..	4 6	..	..	5 25	..	5 35	..	6 39	..	9 3	1026	12 4	..	..	..	2 24	5 36	9 13	1030
13	Culcheth	6 26	7 33	8 15	8 38	1039	12 9	..	1 10	..	2 27	..	4 9	..	5 26	5 28	..	5 38	5 45	6 43	7 45	9 6	1029	12 7	..	6 21	8 3	2 27	5 39	9 16	1033
15	Lowton St. Mary's .... arr	6 30	7 38	8 19	8 42	1043	12 14	..	1 14	..	2 31	..	4 14	..	5 30	5 32	..	5 42	5 50	6 47	7 49	9 10	1033	12 11	..	6 25	8 7	2 31	5 43	9 20	1037
—	Lowton St. Mary's ..dep	6 31	7 39	8 21	L 5	1044	..	1220	1 15	..	2 32	3 26	4 16	..	5 31	5 33	..	5 44	..	6 49	7 50	9 11	1034	12 12	..	6 26	8 8	2 32	5 44	9 21	1038
16¾	West Leigh B	6 35	..	8 25	9 9	1048	..	1224	1 19	..	2 36	3 30	4 20	..	5 35	5 37	..	5 48	..	6 54	7 54	9 15	1038	..	..	..	..	..	..	..	..
18	Bickershaw C	6 39	..	8 29	9 13	1052	..	1228	1 23	..	2 40	3 34	4 24	..	5 39	5 41	..	5 52	..	6 59	..	9 19	1042	..	..	..	..	..	..	..	..
19	Hindley & Platt Bridge ..	6 42	7 47	8 32	9 16	1055	..	1231	1 26	..	2 43	3 38	4 27	..	5 42	5 44	..	5 56	..	7 3	7 59	9 22	1045	..	..	6 34	8 16	2 40	5 52	9 29	1046
20¾	Lower Ince	6 46	7 51	8 36	9 20	1059	..	1235	1 30	..	2 47	3 42	4 31	..	5 46	5 48	..	6 0	..	7 8	8 3	9 26	1049	..	..	6 38	8 20	2 44	5 56	9 33	1050
21¾	Wigan (Central) ..... arr	6 49	7 54	8 39	9 23	11 2	..	1238	1 33	..	2 50	3 45	4 34	..	5 49	5 51	..	6 3	..	7 11	8 6	9 29	1052	12 23	..	6 41	8 23	2 47	5 59	9 36	1053
—	Lowton St. Mary's ..... dep	..	..	..	8 44	..	..	..	..	1 20	..	..	..	4 22	..	..	..	..	..	..	..	..	..	..	..	..	..	..	..	..	..
7	Golborne (North)	..	..	..	8 49	..	..	..	..	1 24	..	..	..	4 27	..	..	..	..	..	..	..	..	..	..	..	..	..	..	..	..	..
8¾	Ashton-in-Makerfield	..	..	..	8 53	..	..	..	..	1 28	..	..	..	4 31	..	..	..	..	..	..	..	..	..	..	..	..	..	..	..	..	..
10¾	Haydock	..	..	..	8 57	..	..	..	..	1 32	..	..	..	4 35	..	..	..	..	..	..	..	..	..	..	..	..	..	..	..	..	..
13¾	St. Helens Central ... arr	..	..	..	9 4	..	..	..	..	1 38	..	..	..	4 41	..	..	..	..	..	..	..	..	..	..	..	..	..	..	..	..	..

Miles		Week Days																									Sundays					
		a.m	am	am	am	a.m	a.m	a.m	a.m	a.m. S		p.m S	p.m E	p.m S	p.m L	p.m	p.m E	p.m S	p.m	pm	p.m E	p.m	p.m	p.m	p.m S		a.m	a.m	p.m	p.m	p.m	
—	St. Helens Central ..dep	..	..	..	..	7 5	..	..	9 35	..	..	..	..	..	1 59	..	..	..	4 52	..	..	..	..	..	..	..	..	..	..	..	..	..
3	Haydock	..	..	..	..	7 12	..	..	9 42	..	..	..	..	..	2 6	..	..	..	4 59	..	..	..	..	..	..	..	..	..	..	..	..	..
4¾	Ashton-in-Makerfield	..	..	..	..	7 17	..	..	9 47	..	..	..	..	..	2 11	..	..	..	5 4	..	..	..	..	..	..	..	..	..	..	..	..	..
6¾	Golborne (North)	..	..	..	..	7 21	..	..	9 51	..	..	..	..	..	2 15	..	..	..	5 8	..	..	..	..	..	..	..	..	..	..	..	..	..
8¾	Lowton St. Mary's ..... arr	..	..	..	..	7 25	..	..	9 55	..	..	..	..	..	2 19	..	..	..	5 12	..	..	..	..	..	..	..	..	..	..	..	..	..
—	Mls Wigan (Central) ... dep	5 4	610	621	634	..	8 4	9 10	..	11 30	..	..	1 0	1 15	1 48	3 40	..	..	..	5 5	..	7 38	9 5	9 22	11 12	..	5 15	7 0	1233	4 41	9 0	..
—	¾ Lower Ince	5 8	613	624	637	..	8 7	9 13	..	11 33	..	..	1 3	1 18	1 51	3 43	..	..	..	5 8	..	7 41	9 8	9 25	11 15	..	5 18	7 3	1236	4 44	9 3	..
—	2¾ Hindley & Platt Bridge	5 12	617	628	642	..	8 11	9 17	..	11 37	..	..	1 7	1 22	1 55	3 47	..	..	..	512	..	7 45	9 12	9 29	11 19	..	5 22	7 7	1 0	4 48	9 7	..
—	3¾ Bickershaw C	5S16	..	631	..	..	8 14	9 20	..	11 40	..	..	1 10	1 25	1 58	3 50	..	..	..	515	..	7 48	9 15	9 32	11 22	..	..	..	..	..	..	..
—	4¾ West Leigh B	5 20	622	635	..	..	8 18	9 24	..	11 44	..	..	1 14	1 29	2 2	3 54	..	..	..	519	..	7 55	9 19	9 36	11 26	..	..	..	..	..	..	..
—	6¾ Lowton St. Mary's arr	5 24	625	639	..	..	8 22	9 27	..	11 48	..	..	1 18	1 33	2L6	3 58	..	..	..	522	..	7 59	9 23	9 39	11 30	..	5 29	7 15	1 6	4 53	9 12	..
—	Lowton St. Mary's .... dep	5 25	626	639	..	7 26	8 23	9 28	9 56	11 49	..	1240	1 19	1 34	2 20	..	4 0	4 35	..	527	7 0	8 2	9 25	9 40	11 31	..	5 30	7 16	1 7	4 56	9 15	..
10¼	Culcheth	5 30	633	644	655	7 31	8 28	9 33	10 1	11 54	..	1246	1 24	1 39	2 25	..	4 9	4 40	..	528	7 5	8 8	9 30	9 45	11 36	..	5 35	7 21	1 12	5 1	9 20	..
11½	Newchurch Halt	5 33	636	647	..	7 34	8 31	9 36	10 4	11 57	..	1249	1 27	1 42	2 28	..	4 12	4 43	..	531	7 8	..	9 33	9 48	..	..	..	..	1 15	5 4	9 23	..
14	Glazebrook .... arr	5 38	..	653	7 1	7 39	8 36	9 40	10 10	12 2	..	1255	1 32	1 47	2 32	..	4 17	..	..	536	7 12	8 13	9 38	..	11 42	..	..	..	..	5 10	9 29	..
15	Irlam and Cadishead "	5 43	647	..	7 6	7 43	8 40	9 45	10H37	12 6	..	1 0	1 36	1 52	2 37	..	4 22	4 52	..	541	7 18	8 18	9 44	9 56	11 46	..	5 43	7 29	1 23	5 15	9 34	..
20½	Trafford Park A .... "	6Y33	7 8	..	715	8Y 6	9Y10	10 1	10H52	12Y36	..	1 15	2Y10	2Y30	2 53	..	5Y 0	5Y38	..	557	7Y40	8 34	10 0	10Y47	..	..	6Y51	8Y35	2Y45	5 30	9 49	..
23½	Manchester (Central) "	6Y40	715	..	722	8Y15	9Y18	10 8	10H59	12Y43	..	1 23	2Y17	2Y37	2 59	..	5Y 7	5Y45	..	6 4	7Y47	8 41	10 7	10Y54	12H15	..	6Y58	8Y13	1Y44	5 37	9 56	..

A Trafford Park and Stretford
A Dep. 4 13 p.m. on Fridays
B West Leigh and Bedford
C Bickershaw and Abram
E Except Saturdays.
H Change at Glazebrook

K Change at Irlam and Glazebrook
L or L Change at Lowton St. Mary's to and from Wigan branch line stations
S or S Saturdays only
Y Change at Irlam

For **LOCAL TRAINS** and **intermediate Stations** between Manchester and Glazebrook see Table 151

For **OTHER TRAINS**

BETWEEN	TABLES
Manchester and Wigan	148, 156
Manchester and St. Helens	149

A timetable for services over the Great Central route from Glazebrook to Wigan and St Helen's.

The Midland Railway station at Didsbury, on the line from Manchester Central to Derby.

Garston station, on the CLC line from Manchester Central to Liverpool Central. In March 1861, after the GNR had been using LNWR tracks to reach Garston, a meeting was held to support the Garston and Liverpool Railway. Captain Mark Huish gave support to the scheme against his old company (one wonders why they fired him) and an Act was obtained on 17 May 1861, with powers to make a terminus at Brunswick Dock being given the following year. Opening took place on 1 June 1864 and intermediate stations were sited at Mersey Road, Otters Pool and St Michaels. Another station, Cressington & Grassendale, was opened in 1873 to serve a private estate. The CLC was formed on 5 July 1865 and assumed control of this line.

Table 151 **MANCHESTER and GLAZEBROOK**

Week Days

Miles		a.m A	am	am	am C	am	am	am	am	am C	a.m	am	am	am	a.m E	a.m S	a.m S	p.m	p.m S B	p.m	p.m S	p.m E	p.m	p.m	pm	pm S
—	Manchester (Cen.).dep	5 18	530	..	6 0	620	650	710	720	735	7 38	8 0	835	933	1040	1110	..	12 7	1215	1233	1255	1255	1 11	1 35	..	2 0
3	Trafford Park & Stret-	5 24	536	..	6 6	626	657	716	726	..	7 44	8 6	841	939	1046	1116	1141	12 13	..	1239	1 1	1 1	1 17	1 41	..	2 6
5	Urmston ....[ford	5 29	541	..	611	631	7 2	721	731	..	7 49	811	846	944	1051	1121	1146	12 18	1224	1244	1 6	1 6	1 22	1 46	..	210
5½	Chassen Road..........	5 31	544	..	613	633	7 5	723	733	..	7 51	813	848	946	1053	1123	1148	12 20	..	1246	1 8	1 8	1 24	1 48	..	212
6¼	Flixton	5 36	548	..	616	637	7 9	727	736	..	7 54	817	852	949	1056	1126	1151	12 23	1228	1250	1 11	1 11	1 27	1 51	..	215
8½	Irlam and Cadishead...	5 45	554	613	621	642	716	733	741	750	8 0	825	858	955	11 1	1131	1157	12 28	1233	1255	1 16	1 16	1 32	1 56	214	220
9½	Glazebrook........ arr	..	558	617	..	650	721	737	..	..	8 4	829	9 2	959	11 5	..	12 2	12F32	..	1 0	1 20	..	..	2 1	218	224

Week Days—*continued*

	p.m	p.m	p.m E	pm	p.m E	pm S	pm S	p.m E	pm E	p.m E	p.m E	p.m	p.m E	pm	pm	p.m	p.m	p.m	p.m	p.m	p.m	p.m	p.m	p.m S	
Manchester (Cen.).dep	2 35	3 33	4 5	..	4 37	445	..	4 57	..	..	5 12	5 33	5 45	6 5	635	7 12	7 40	8 30	9 10	9 40	..	1015	1045	..	..
Trafford Park & Stret-	2 42	3 39	4H11	..	4 44	451	..	5 5	..	5 12	5 19	5 40	5 52	611	642	7 18	7 46	8 36	9 16	9 46	..	1021	1051	..	..
Urmston ....[ford	2 47	3 44	4H16	..	4 49	456	..	..	..	5 17	5 25	5 47	5 58	616	647	7 23	7 51	8 41	9 23	9 51	..	1026	1056	..	..
Chassen Road...........	2 49	3 46	4H19	..	4 52	458	..	..	..	5 20	5 27	5 50	6 1	618	650	7 25	7 53	8 43	9 25	9 53	..	1028	1059	..	..
Flixton	2 52	3 50	4H23	..	4 56	5 1	..	..	..	5 25	5 30	5 55	6 4	622	653	7 29	7 56	8 47	9 29	9 57	..	1031	11 2	..	..
Irlam and Cadishead...	2 57	3 56	4H29	452	5 2	5 6	515	5 18	525	5 32	5L46	6 2	6 10	628	658	7 35	8 1	8 53	9F45	10 3	1016	1036	11 7	1154	..
Glazebrook........ arr	3E 1	4 0	..	457	..	..	519	5 22	529	5 38	5 52	6 6	..	633	..	7 39	8 5	8 57	9 49	10 7	1020	1040	1111	1158	..

Sundays

	a.m A	a.m	a.m	a.m	a.m	a.m		a.m C	a.m		p.m	p.m C	p.m	p.m	p.m	p.m	p.m	p.m	p.m	p.m C	p.m	p.m	
Manchester (Cen.).dep	5 25	..	7 0	7 25	..	8 30	..	10 0	1120	..	1255	1 15	..	2 8	4 50	5 5	7 10	8 25	8 42	9 20	9 57	1025	..
Trafford Park & Stret-	5 31	..	7 6	7 31	..	8 36	..	..	1126	..	1 1	..	..	2 14	4 56	5 11	7 16	..	8 48	9 26	10 3	1031	..
Urmston ....[ford	5 36	..	7 11	7 36	..	8 41	..	1010	1131	..	1 6	..	..	2 19	5 1	5 16	7 21	..	8 53	9 31	10 8	1036	..
Chassen Road...........	5 38	..	7 13	7 38	..	8 43	..	..	1133	..	1 8	..	..	2 21	5 3	5 18	7 23	..	8 55	9 33	1010	1038	..
Flixton...................	5 41	..	7 16	7 41	..	8 46	..	..	1136	..	1 11	..	..	2 24	5 6	5 21	7 26	..	8 58	9 36	1013	1041	..
Irlam and Cadishead...	5 46	6 13	7 21	7 46	7 55	8 51	..	1017	1141	..	1 16	1 28	2 15	2 29	5 13	5 27	7 31	..	9 4	9 41	1020	1046	..
Glazebrook........ arr	..	6 16	7 25	..	7 58	8 55	..	..	1145	..	..	..	2 19	2 33	5 17	5 31	7 35	8 40	9 8	..	1024	1050	..

Week Days

Miles		a.m	a.m	a.m	a.m E	a.m S	a.m D	a.m	am	am	a.m	a.m	a.m	a.m C	am	am	am	a.m	am	a.m	a.m	a.m	p.m S	p.m S	p.m S
—	Glazebrook ....dep	..	5 39	..	6 36	6 39	..	7 2	713	..	7 40	7 46	7 57	..	817	..	837	8 53	921	9 41	1033	1118	12 3	..	1241
1	Irlam and Cadishead...	5 13	5 43	6 17	6 40	6 43	6 50	7 6	719	740	7 43	7 52	8 1	8 8	821	832	840	8 55	925	9 45	1037	1122	12 6	1220	1248
3¼	Flixton....................	5 18	..	6 22	6 45	6 48	6 55	..	725	746	..	7 57	8 6	8 14	826	837	..	9 0	930	9 50	1042	1127	..	1225	..
4	Chassen Road	5 21	..	6 25	6 48	6 51	6 58	..	728	749	..	8 0	8 9	8 17	829	840	..	9 3	933	9 53	1045	1130	..	1228	..
4½	Urmston ....[ford	5 24	..	6 28	6 51	6 54	7 2	..	732	752	..	8 3	8 12	8 20	833	843	..	9 5	935	9 56	1047	1132	..	1231	1256
6½	Trafford Park & Stret-	5 29	..	6 33	6 56	7 0	7 8	7 15	738	757	..	8 8	8 18	8 28	839	848	..	9 10	940	10 1	1052	1137	..	1236	..
9¼	Manchester (Cen.). arr	5 35	..	6 40	7 3	7 7	7 15	7 22	745	8 4	..	8 15	8 25	8 33	846	855	..	9 18	947	10 8	1059	1145	..	1243	1 6

Week Days—*continued*

	p.m E	p.m S	p.m	p.m N	p.m E	p.m S	p.m	pm	p.m	pm E	p.m	p.m E	p.m E	p.m S	pm	p.m C	pm	p.m E	p.m S	p.m E	p.m E	pm	p.m C	pm	p.m E
Glazebrook.......dep	1243	125[illegible]	1S24	1 33	..	..	2 33	..	3 47	418	4 40	..	..	5 18	537	--	..	6 29	6 53	7 13	7 21	..	..	814	8 43
Irlam and Cadishead...	1253	1 0	1 28	1 36	1 55	2 15	2 37	315	3 52	422	4 44	..	5 22	5 22	541	6 10	620	6 36	6 57	7 18	7 25	744	8 10	818	8 47
Flixton....................	1258	1 5	1 33	..	2 0	2 20	2 42	320	3 57	..	4 49	..	5 27	5 27	546	..	625	6 41	7 2	..	7 30	749	..	823	8 52
Chassen Road	1 1	1 8	1 36	..	2 3	2 23	2 45	323	4 0	..	4 52	..	5 30	5 30	549	..	628	6 44	7 5	..	7 33	752	..	826	8 55
Urmston ....[ford	1 4	1 10	1 39	..	2 5	2 25	2 48	325	4 3	..	4 54	..	5 33	5 33	552	..	630	6 47	7 7	..	7 35	755	..	829	8 57
Trafford Park & Stret-	1 9	1 15	1 44	..	2 10	2 30	2 53	330	4 9	..	5 0	5 11	5 38	5 38	557	..	635	6 52	7 12	..	7 40	8 0	..	834	9 2
Manchester (Cen.). arr	1 16	1 23	1 51	..	2 17	2 37	2 59	337	4 16	..	5 7	5 18	5 45	5 45	6 4	6 25	642	7 0	7 19	..	747	8 7	8 25	841	9 9

Week Days—*continued* / **Sundays**

	p.m	p.m	p.m	p.m	p.m S	p.m		a.m A	a.m C	a.m	a.m	p.m	p.m	p.m	p.m	p.m	p.m	p.m	p.m	p.m	p.m	p.m	
Glazebrook........dep	9 20	9 39	1028	11 18	1143	1152	..	..	..	..	9 38	1226	1 26	2 26	4 41	5 11	6 10	6 41	8 54	9 30	1016	1121	..
Irlam and Cadishead...	9 25	9 44	1032	..	1146	..	..	6 36	7 59	8 20	9 42	1230	1 30	2 30	4 45	5 15	6 14	6 45	8 58	9 34	1020	1125	..
Flixton..................	9 30	9 49	1037	..	..	12S0	..	6 41	..	8 25	9 47	1235	..	2 35	4 50	5 20	6 19	6 50	9 3	9 39	1025	1130	..
Chassen Road..........	9 33	9 52	1040	..	..	..	..	6 44	..	8 28	9 50	1238	..	2 38	4 53	5 23	6 22	6 53	9 6	9 42	1028	..	..
Urmston..........[ford	9 36	9 55	1042	11S28	..	12 5	..	6 46	..	8 30	9 52	1240	..	2 40	4 55	5 25	6 24	6 55	9 8	9 44	1030	1134	..
Trafford Park & Stret-	9 41	10 0	1047	..	..	..	..	6 51	..	8 35	9 57	1245	..	2 45	5 0	5 30	6 29	7 0	9 13	9 49	1035	1139	..
Manchester (Cen.)..arr	9 48	10 7	1054	11N33	..	1215	..	6 58	8 13	8 42	10 4	1252	1 44	2 52	5 7	5 37	6 36	7 7	9 20	9 56	1042	1146	..

A To and from Warrington (Table 150) **B** To and from Southport (Table 150a) **C** To and from Liverpool (Table 150)

D From Wigan (Cen.) dep. 6 10 a.m. (Table 149a) **E** or **E** Except Saturdays **F** Arrive 9 34 p.m.

H 2 minutes later on Fridays **L** Arrive 5 36 p.m. **N** or **N** 5 minutes later on Saturdays **S** or **S** Saturdays only

A timetable for CLC trains running between Manchester Central and Glazebrook.

The GC had a sub-shed of Gorton (39A) at Dinting, on the Lancashire/Derbyshire border, near Glossop. In 1954 the little shed was home to three ex-Great Central Railway *Robinson* J11 5 ft 1 in 0–6–0s. When Dinting shed closed in the mid-1960s, a group took it over for use as a steam museum and by 1982 it had a good selection of main line and industrial steam locomotives, as the list below shows:

Main Line locos
LMS 'Jubilee' 4–6–0: 5596 *Bahamas*
LMS 'Royal Scot' 4–6–0: 6115 *Scots Guardsman*
GCR 04 Class 2–8–0: 102
LNWR 'Coal Tank' 0–6–2T: 1054
LNER A2/3 4–6–2: 532 *Blue Peter*
LNER A4 4–6–2: 19 *Bittern*

Industrial locos
RSH 0–4–0OCT: *Southwick*
RSH 0–6–0ST: 150 *Warrington*
Hudswell-Clark 0–6–0T: *Nunlow*
Avonside 0–6–0ST: 1883
Barclay 0–4–0ST: *Tiny*
Avonside/RR 0–4–0D: RS8
McEwan Pratt (petrol loco): *Jacob*

This photograph shows LMS 'Jubilee' loco no. 5690 *Leander* and ex-SR 4–4–0 no. 30925

Another view of *Leander* at Dinting.

Ex-LMS 'Royal Scot' 4–6–0 *Scots Guardsman* at Dinting.

Ex-LNER A2 Pacific *Blue Peter* inside Dinting shed, with ex-LNWR 0–6–2 'Coal Tank' to her right, and A4 Pacific *Bittern* is just in view, on the extreme right.

Ex-GCR 2–8–0 no. 102 is at the door of Dinting shed. The Dinting operation had the unfortunate tag of being the first preservation operation to close in the early 1990s.

MORECAMBE AND HEYSHAM

The coastal town of Morecambe was developed by the Midland Railway, in conjunction with the (Little) North Western Railway, as a holiday resort, but it became famous as a packet port for steamers to Belfast and the Isle of Man. By the turn of the century, silting problems at Morecambe led the railway company to develop a new port to the south at Heysham where sailings to Belfast commenced in 1904.

Morecambe retained its role as a holiday resort after the packet boats left its port, the Midland Railway bringing visitors and holidaymakers over the Pennines from Yorkshire. The LNWR showed interest in a line to Morecambe in the 1860s, opening a station in the town in August 1864, but the Midland Railway was always the more important company here.

When Heysham Harbour was opened, the Midland Railway began a passenger service between here and Morecambe on 11 July 1904, using steam railmotors. The line was electrified in 1908, the first electric services operating from 13 April. Unusually, the line used a 25 cycle 6600 volt AC overhead system, instead of third rail operation which was then the most common system in use. This system was to prove useful to BR when experimenting with electrification for the West Coast Main Line. This line, which had been extended to Lancaster in 1906, was converted to 25kv operation between October 1955 and March 1956 and used as a test-bed for evaluation of this high voltage system which had been a great success in France. Only a year after experiments began on this modest ex-MR line, electrification of the WCML using the 25 kv system began on the Manchester–Crewe section, bringing about a transformation in rail travel when work on the WCML was completed.

Morecambe (Promenade) station, opened by the Midland Railway on 24 March 1907 to replace their original station at Northumberland Street, which closed at the same time. Morecambe was put on the railway map when a station simply called Morecambe was opened by the MR and (Little) North Western Railway in August 1850 to serve the, as yet undeveloped, Morecambe Harbour. A grand harbour scheme had been planned in 1848 but it never grew to the size that had been envisaged. At the same time both railway companies made great efforts to develop the area as a holiday resort, its main assets being the wide bays and views of the Lake District. The area had been popular as a bathing place since the early nineteenth century, centred on a small village called Poulton-le-Sands with a daily coach from Lancaster serving the place. The port was no more than a wooden jetty when cargo vessels began using it in 1851. In the same year, the steamer *Albion* began to operate a passenger service across the bay between Morecambe and Piel Pier, which had been opened by the Furness Railway in 1846. A year later, the Belfast Steam Packet Company began sailings to Morecambe from Belfast and a stone jetty was built to carry passenger trains, which ran until 1857. The two railway companies began a Morecambe–Belfast steamer service in 1853, using two small steamers, *Laurel* and *Artubus* from 1854. Ten years later, from 8 August, the LNWR began train services to Morecambe from Euston, to its own station at Morecambe (Poulton Lane). Steamers still sailed to Ireland up until 1903, but the MR noted that the harbour was silting up in 1896 and plans were made to move the port to Heysham. The town still retained its role as a holiday resort, and trains carry visitors right up to the present day.

The station concourse at Heysham, opened when sailings started from the newly established port in 1904. Steamer sailings to Belfast began on 1 September 1904 using three ships of 2,000 tons, *Antrim*, *Donegal* and *Londonderry*. Each night the boat for Belfast left Heysham at 11 p.m., a boat train having left St Pancras at 5 p.m. to connect with it, calling at all stations of importance en route. A boat service to Douglas, on the Isle of Man, began on 1 June 1905 and an express for this service left St Pancras at 8.30 a.m., giving a Douglas arrival time of 5.15 p.m. A local train service began between Morecambe and Heysham on 11 July 1904, and an electric service began on 13 April 1908. Boat services to Belfast ended on the Heysham route on 6 April 1975 when Stranraer became the main port for Northern Ireland sailings, and passenger trains stopped running between Morecambe and Heysham on 8 October 1975. A local service between Lancaster and Morecambe still operates, with two midday services running through to Heysham.

Table 23

EXPRESS SERVICES BETWEEN

LONDON, MANCHESTER, LEEDS and BELFAST via Heysham

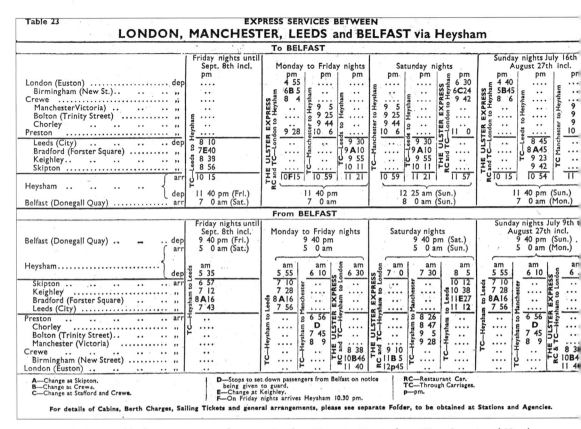

To BELFAST

	Friday nights until Sept. 8th incl.	Monday to Friday nights			Saturday nights			Sunday nights July 16th August 27th incl.		
	pm	pm	pm	pm	pm	pm	pm	pm	pm	pm
London (Euston) .... dep	....	4 55	....	....	....	....	6 30	4 40	....	....
Birmingham (New St.).. ,,	..	6B 5	....	....	....	....	6C24	5B45	....	..
Crewe .... ,,	..	8 4	....	....	....	....	9 42	8 6	....	9
Manchester Victoria) .. ,,	..	....	9 5	....	9 5	....	....	....	....	9
Bolton (Trinity Street) ... ,,	....	....	9 25	....	9 25	....	....	....	....	9
Chorley .. .. .. ,,	..	....	9 44	....	9 44	....	....	....	....	9
Preston .... ,,	....	9 28	10 6	....	10 6	....	11 0	....	....	10
Leeds (City) .... dep	8 10	..	..	9 30	....	9 30	....	....	8 45	..
Bradford (Forster Square) .. ,,	7E40	..	..	9A10	....	9A10	....	....	8 A45	..
Keighley.. .. .. ,,	8 39	..	..	9 55	....	9 55	....	....	9 23	..
Skipton .... ,,	8 56	..	..	10 11	....	10 11	....	....	9 42	..
Heysham .. .. .. arr	10 15	10F15	10 59	11 21	10 59	11 21	11 57	10 15	10 54	11
Heysham .. .. .. dep	11 40 pm (Fri.)	11 40 pm			12 25 am (Sun.)			11 40 pm (Sun.)		
Belfast (Donegall Quay) ...... arr	7 0 am (Sat.)	7 0 am			8 0 am (Sun.)			7 0 am (Mon.)		

Column labels: THE ULSTER EXPRESS RC and TC—London to Heysham; TC—Manchester to Heysham; TC—Leeds to Heysham.

From BELFAST

	Friday nights until Sept. 8th incl.	Monday to Friday nights			Saturday nights			Sunday nights July 9th August 27th incl.		
Belfast (Donegall Quay) .. dep	9 40 pm (Fri.)	9 40 pm			9 40 pm (Sat.)			9 40 pm (Sun.)		
Belfast (Donegall Quay) .. arr	5 0 am (Sat.)	5 0 am			5 0 am (Sun.)			5 0 am (Mon.)		
	am	am	am	am	am	am	am	am	am	am
Heysham ...... dep	5 35	5 55	6 10	6 30	7 0	7 30	8 5	5 55	6 10	6
Skipton .. .. .. arr	6 57	7 10	....	....	....	....	10 12	7 10	....	..
Keighley .. .. .. ,,	7 12	7 28	....	....	....	....	10 38	7 28	....	..
Bradford (Forster Square) .. ,,	8A16	8A16	....	....	....	....	11E27	8A16	....	..
Leeds (City) .... arr	7 43	7 56	....	....	....	....	11 12	7 56	....	..
Preston .. .. .. arr	....	....	6 56	....	8 26	....	....	....	6 56	..
Chorley .. .. .. ,,	....	....	D	....	8 47	....	....	....	D	..
Bolton (Trinity Street).. ,,	....	....	7 45	....	9 5	....	....	....	7 45	..
Manchester (Victoria) .... ,,	....	....	8 9	....	9 28	....	....	....	8 9	..
Crewe .. .. .. ,,	....	....	8 38	....	9 10	....	....	....	8 38	..
Birmingham (New Street) .... ,,	....	....	10B46	....	....	....	11B5	....	10B4	
London (Euston) .. .. ,,	....	....	11 40	....	....	....	12p45	....	11 4	

Column labels: TC—Heysham to Leeds; TC—Heysham to Manchester; THE ULSTER EXPRESS RC and TC—Heysham to London; TC—Heysham to London.

A—Change at Skipton.
B—Change at Crewe.
C—Change at Stafford and Crewe.
D—Stops to set down passengers from Belfast on notice being given to guard.
E—Change at Keighley.
F—On Friday nights arrives Heysham 10.30 pm.
RC—Restaurant Car.
TC—Through Carriages.
p—pm.

For details of Cabins, Berth Charges, Sailing Tickets and general arrangements, please see separate Folder, to be obtained at Stations and Agencies.

A 1950s timetable for trains running between London (Euston), Birmingham (New Street) and Heysham to connect with boats for Belfast. Sadly, these trains have now long gone.

SECTION SIX

THE LIVERPOOL OVERHEAD RAILWAY

Serving the busy and congested Liverpool docks, the Overhead Railway was a novel solution to difficulties encountered in this area. It was very similar to American systems operating in New York and Chicago, but was unique in Britain and was the first railway in the country to adopt electric traction. Opened by ex-Prime Minister Lord Salisbury on 4 February 1893, the first section of the railway ran from Herculanium Dock to Alexandra, its primary role being to transport dock workers, seamen, shipping clerks and others who had business in the port. However, the railway also became an excursion route for people to view the 'great liners' which were docked in Liverpool. The railway was extended north to Seaforth Sands on 30 April 1894 and south to Dingle, opening 21 December 1896. The latter section went underground to reach the terminus. Only two years after reaching Dingle, Liverpool Corporation introduced electric tramcars between the city centre and the LOR's southern terminus. From that time, the railway had to fight road competition for the remainder of its existence.

The line reflected the economic situation as the twentieth century progressed. In 1900 10 million passengers were carried but by 1907 numbers had declined to 9 million, falling still further to 8 million in 1909 as a trade slump set in. Passenger numbers increased during the First World War, culminating in an all-time record of 17 million in 1919. The Great Depression of the 1930s saw levels fall to only 5½ million in 1933, but the Second World War increased numbers back to around 14 million. After the war business declined again, as bus competition swallowed up passengers from the railway, and dock traffic decreased. Costly renewals required on the overhead system, decline of the docks, combined with the movement of industry and population away from the centre of Liverpool, sealed the fate of the railway. It closed on 31 December 1956 and was completely demolished the following year. Thus, a unique railway line was lost to Liverpool and the nation.

The Liverpool Overhead Railway, bottom left, passes the site of the Liver Building, where the foundations are just being laid. The site of the new structure is marked by a sign stating that this is to be the new office block for the Royal Liver Friendly Society. The Pier Head lies in the background, with the River Mersey beyond. The necessity for a passenger line serving the docks in Liverpool was recognized as early as 1852 and, in 1878, the Mersey Docks & Harbour Board presented a Bill for a 5¼ mile elevated line. Initially, a single line with passing places was planned, but the Board of Trade objected and plans were modified to provide a double track railway, approved in 1882. Local businessmen took over powers from the MD & HB by an Act of 24 July 1888, and the first section of line opened in 1893, trains being electrically operated. Its signalling was automatically operated, equipment being supplied by the Westinghouse Company, the first railway in Great Britain to use such a system. From 1921 colour lights replaced semaphores then in use.

The Overhead Railway and St Nicholas's Church, with the railway's greatest competitor, the electric tram, at the same location. Such was the damage done to passenger receipts, that exceptionally cheap fares were offered by the LOR company by 1932. Return journeys over the whole line could be bought for 9*d* third class and 1*s* first class. On weekday evenings and Saturday afternoons passengers could travel from either of the railway's termini to any station for only 2*d*. During the Second World War the railway suffered much damage during the blitz of 1940–1, but was always quickly repaired.

Pier Head, Liverpool, with the LOR in the background. When the national railway system came under state control during the Second World War, the LOR was not included. The same also applied when the 1947 Transport Act, which was to bring the railways into state ownership, came into effect, and the LOR continued on as a private concern right up to closure. After the war passenger numbers declined steadily until the line was finally closed in 1956.

A late nineteenth-century view of the docks area in Liverpool, with the Liverpool Overhead Railway on the left.

The same location in the 1920s. Steam lorries, one of which is visible in the distance close to the railway, are beginning to replace horses and carts, and electric trams are taking more passengers from the LOR. On the railway itself a train is approaching Pier Head station.

A very busy scene at Pier Head in the Edwardian period. Several horses and carts fill the road with sacks of merchandise and an early threat to this and other railways in Lancashire, a motor car, is on the front right of the picture. At this time its owner would have been very well-to-do, probably a merchant or even a ship owner. The LOR is on the left; one of its semaphore signals is visible on the bridge in the 'off' position which indicates a train is due.

The LOR in the 1950s, not long before closure. In the background is the Liver Building, still a landmark in Liverpool, with the Pier Head bus terminus just in front of it, providing further evidence of the decline of the railway. Motor lorries and cars predominate in the streets; a sharp contrast to the horses and carts in previous views.

The LOR on its approach to Pier Head in the 1920s. Trams and motor cars predominate, although horses and carts are still in use, two of which can be seen in the foreground.

The LOR in the 1950s with the Liver Building on the right and the offices of the Cunard Shipping Company behind. On the far right is Pier Head with buses approaching the terminus. Private motor cars and lorries litter the street close to the LOR's station.

The modern building of the Liverpool Dock Offices next to the Liver Building in the 1950s, with the LOR in the left foreground.

The LOR with the Dock Offices on the left and Liver Building on the extreme right. The gap in between the two would soon be occupied by the Cunard Building. This view would have been taken just after the First World War, and the LNWR has an advertisement for cheap excursions to North Wales and Blackpool.

The LOR at Pier Head in the 1920s.

A train on the LOR near Pier Head, with semaphore signal clearly in view. The crowded street below gives ample reason for the need to build the railway as a means of rapid passenger transit in the late nineteenth century.

An early twentieth-century view of Pier Head, with the LOR in the background. The scene shows a great number of horses and carriages, provided for the gentry no doubt, and a new electric tram waits in the centre foreground.

One of the LOR's wooden-bodied electric passenger trains, which ran on the three-rail system. The conductor rail was at the side of the track and the current was picked up by a shoe on the offside of the train.

A busy scene at Liverpool Docks after the arrival of the ocean liner *Aquitania*. Many passengers on the LOR used the railway to view these magnificent ships lying at anchor in the Port of Liverpool.

LOCOMOTIVE-BUILDING LANCASHIRE

While cotton and coal were the staple industries of Lancashire, these were not the only activities that the county was involved in. Within Lancashire, several engineering firms were established, many specializing in locomotive construction. Among these were some famous companies, such as Sharp-Stewart and Beyer-Peacock, who produced engines for export to all parts of the British Empire and beyond, as well as supplying locos to industrial railways all over the British Isles. These private companies also built locomotives for the main line railways at times when demand exceeded the capacity of main line company works to produce sufficient engines to meet needs. In the early days of the main lines these private companies made their names building engines for embryo companies to run trains over the new main line routes, until they could start building their own.

The majority of these private locomotive builders either went out of business or diversified into other areas of engineering by the late 1960s, and a great source of skills and foreign revenue was lost to the nation. However, many of the products of these firms are still in existence, either in preservation or at the head of service trains in places like India, as testament to the quality and reliability of these engines.

The erecting shop at the Beyer-Peacock works in Manchester. The company was established in 1854 by Charles Beyer, Richard Peacock and Henry Robertson to build railway locomotives. Much of the company's production was exported to countries in the Empire, and engines for export to India are being built in this view. This company also built for the home market, including the main line companies. Indeed, LMS diesel shunters which were introduced in the 1930s were actually built by the Dick Kerr Works at Preston.

Narrow gauge 2–4–0 loco *Blanche*, built by Sharp-Stewart Ltd at its Atlas Works, Manchester. The engine was built in 1882 for the Penrhyn Slate Quarries, Bethesda, North Wales. It weighed 22 tons, had 3½ ft diameter driving wheels and 2½ ft diameter leading wheels. The engine worked for many years on the Penrhyn Quarry railway and was purchased for preservation in the 1950s when the quarry railway was closed. The loco is still in existence and still runs, heading passenger trains on the Ffestiniog Railway between Blaenau Ffestiniog and Porthmadog in North Wales. The loco is testament to the quality of work produced by these private engine builders.

A small 0–4–0 tank engine built by Sharp-Stewart for the South American market.

A class 885 2–6–0 tank engine with 14 in outside cylinders, 2 ft 9 in driving wheels and 1 ft 10 in bogie wheels built by Sharp-Stewart for a company in Chile, who named it *Pizarro*. The loco was built in 1887 and weighed 24 tons in working order, with a tank capacity of 600 gallons.

Another Sharp-Stewart 2–6–0, named *Uladislao Frias*, for the South American market.

Sharp-Stewart South American 2–4–0, built for a narrow gauge system, with 3 ft 10 in driving wheels and 2ft 3 in leading wheels. It weighed 20½ tons in working order.

Sharp-Stewart narrow gauge 4–4–0 for South America with 4 ft 7 in drivers and 2ft 6 in truck wheels. Its total weight was 19¼ tons.

Another Sharp-Stewart engine for South America. This narrow gauge 0–6–0 had 3 ft driving wheels and weighed 17½ tons.

Loco no. 18 *Parnahyba*, built in 1886 for a South American narrow gauge mountain railway. This 4–4–0 had 3¾ ft diameter driving wheels and 29 in bogie wheels, with a total weight of 19½ tons. It was a member of the company's 872 class.

Sharp-Stewart narrow gauge 4–6–0 no. 21 *Goyaz* for South America. The loco weighed 23 tons and had 3 ft 4 in drivers and 2ft 2 in leading wheels.

Sharp-Stewart 2–6–2 tank loco, built for a South American railway. It weighed 29 tons, had 36 in drivers and 26 in truck wheels and was designed for railways with tight curves. This engine, no. 1 *Ouro Preto*, could haul loads of up to 1,000 tons.

Narrow gauge 2–4–0 tank loco MNR no. 2 built by Sharp-Stewart in 1882. Its total weight was 17¾ tons and had 3 ft 9 in drivers and 2 ft 9 in leading wheels.

A small Sharp-Stewart South American 0–6–0 tank loco.

Sharp-Stewart 0–4–0 saddle tank *Atlas*, built for the Darjeeling Himalayan Railway, India in 1870. This 24 in gauge loco had 26 in drivers and weighed 10¾ tons. It was capable of hauling 600 tons on level ground.

A main line engine, built by Sharp-Stewart in 1849 for the Manchester, South Junction & Altrincham Railway which opened in the same year. This 2–2–2 loco, *Flora*, was built at the company's Atlas works, which was situated on the banks of the Rochdale Canal.

A small 0–4–0 saddle tank loco built by Sharpe-Stewart for the British industrial market.

Other companies built railway locos for the British main line system, apart from Sharpe-Stewart, one example of which appears here. This engine was built for the Furness Railway by the Fairbairn Company of Manchester in 1855. It was a 4–4–0 and given the number 9 by the railway company. Note the 'haycock' style firebox, a fairly common feature of main line locomotives in the mid-nineteenth century.

Industrial locomotive *Knighton*, built by Beyer-Peacock in 1861 for the Knighton Railway, as a 0–4–2 saddle tank. The engine cost the railway company some £1,300 and it is posed outside the Beyer-Peacock works.

ACKNOWLEDGEMENTS

We should like to record our thanks to all who have assisted in the preparation of this book, especially Gwyn Roberts, Terry Roberts, Roger Carpenter and 'Tim' Shuttleworth.

BRITAIN IN OLD PHOTOGRAPHS

To order any of these titles please telephone our distributor, Littlehampton Book Services on 01903 721596
For a catalogue of these and our other titles please ring Regina Schinner on 01453 731114